NEW YORK SPLENDOR

NEW YORK SPLENDOR

The City's Most Memorable Rooms

*For Yeonhee Seo.
From a grateful
Wendy Moonan*

Wendy Moonan

FOREWORD BY ROBERT A.M. STERN

RIZZOLI
NEW YORK

New York · Paris · London · Milan

CONTENTS

I OFTEN THINK of Manhattan apartments and town houses as secret gardens, hidden from view by building facades behind which flower personal expressions of great taste and sophistication. As with any garden the plantings come and go, both seasonally and with changes of ownership. That's why it's so wonderful to have so many "secret gardens" captured between the covers of this book.

Between the 1940s and the '70s, interior decoration, previously characterized by a certain dilettantism, underwent a dramatic metamorphosis, emerging as a fully articulated approach not only to the embellishment but also to the actual creation—in effect the architecture—of residential interiors, thereby coming close to fulfilling a long-held goal of modernism: Gesamtkunstwerk, or total work of art. What had been known as decorating since the days of Elsie de Wolfe emerged as interior design, space design, and even interior architecture. Though this transformation began in fin-de-siècle France and Germany and can be traced through the work of Frank Lloyd Wright, as well as that of Walter Gropius, Ludwig Mies van der Rohe, and Le Corbusier—the principal formulators of canonical modernism—the next phase, in which interior design was accepted as a fact of professional practice, was in large measure a New York story. During this period, apartment after apartment in Manhattan's choicest residential neighborhoods was reinvented—drastically reconfigured and redecorated to reflect the tastes and lifestyle patterns of young families who had chosen to root themselves in city life rather than the suburbs. This trend continued as these families matured and others joined in the revival of urban living, transforming apartment interiors—many of them anonymously conceived—into glorious environments and, beginning in the mid-1980s, doing the same with downtown lofts and spaces in other surprising building types like outmoded office towers. For a while the new approach typically implied that one had to tear everything out and paint all the walls white. But that quick fix was not enough for many who wanted to cocoon themselves in carefully orchestrated and detailed environments.

In showcasing a great variety of New York interiors in a beautiful way, Wendy Moonan opens the doors to these private "gardens," sharing them with her readers and amplifying our knowledge of the city's social history. Moonan understands that the criterion for judgment must be quality of vision and execution, rather than the celebration of a particular style; her survey is wonderfully eclectic, constituting a valuable historical record of the trends and movements that swept upper-class New York in the last quarter of the twentieth century and the first decades of the twenty-first, from spare minimalism to Old World opulence and back. Judiciously selecting from the best work by interior designers and architects, with artists thrown into the mix as well, she captures what is in essence ephemeral and creates a compilation that is a pleasure for us to peruse today and that will live on as an invaluable document to inspire future clients, decorators, and historians.

Robert A.M. Stern
New York, New York

INTRODUCTION

A Passion for Interiors, New York–Style

WHEN I WAS GROWING UP in Westport, Connecticut, in the 1960s, no one I knew had a decorator. My father was English, and many of our family friends were European. They had antiques and paintings, but the prevailing wisdom was that people with taste should be able to furnish and design their own interiors. Period.

My, how quickly the pendulum of popular opinion has changed!

As the At Home editor at *Town & Country* in the 1980s, I crisscrossed America scouting and writing about residences that had been decorated by the top figures in the field. Owners were intensely proud about having commissioned Mario Buatta or Denning & Fourcade to reimagine their residences. I wrote about architecture and design in the 1990s for *House & Garden* and in the 2000s for *Architectural Digest*, recording residential style trends that spanned the gamut, from Old World, over-the-top palatial to strictly minimal—and everything in between. I came to admire dozens of architects and designers, and I still follow their careers.

This book is a compendium of my favorite private residential rooms in New York City. It is an eclectic group, ranging from a dramatic, contemporary Tribeca triplex in the shadow of One World Trade Center to a town house in Brooklyn with a living room that could be in the Palace of Versailles.

This book is not meant to be comprehensive or encyclopedic; it is a completely subjective survey of rooms realized between 1970 and 2018. My main criterion was simply that each project have the "wow" factor—rooms that elicited, from me, gasps of pleasure and admiration.

What unifies these spaces is the passion of the talented people who choreographed them. These include the gifted men and women who work to realize clients' dreams. They share a language that is visual. They think in terms of proportion, texture, light, and materials. And they have the professional knowledge, wisdom, experi-

Beginning in 2002, artist Julian Schnabel started taking giant Polaroids of his private rooms in the Palazzo Chupi, a residential tower he created in Greenwich Village. Since he constantly changes the works of art in his home, he likes to record particular moments in the history of a room—here is his living room on the sixth floor of the palazzo in 2008, captured with a rare Polaroid Land camera from the 1970s. Schnabel's passion for art and interiors is clearly evident.

Some of the most beautiful spaces in the book are rooms designers created for themselves. The Park Avenue bedroom that late decorator Mark Hampton made for himself and his wife, Duane, is an example of an elegantly timeless space—it has barely changed in the decades since it was first completed.

ence, and sheer tenacity to translate concepts into reality. To list just a few, they include a legendary architect (Philip Johnson); a master of illusion who worked on sets for stage and screen (Renzo Mongiardino); a preeminent dealer in eighteenth-century European furniture (Helen Fioratti); and a modernist architect and chair of Yale University's School of Architecture (Paul Rudolph).

When experts discuss the psychology of decorating, they write that a positive or negative response to a room is almost always instantaneous. Most people experience a room through their senses and visceral reactions: color; pattern; scale; light; flowers; scented candles; the sensation of silk, linen, wood, or metal; environments that evoke calm, energy, warmth, recognition of home, comfort, or anticipation.

The rooms I have chosen are all about imagination; they invoke a sense of wonder. They start a conversation. How did they get made? What was the concept? Who chose the furniture and art? Some spaces are very grand, others spare or eclectic. The noteworthy rooms include Brooke Astor's iconic library by Parish-Hadley, Gloria Vanderbilt's sublime patchwork bedroom, Lela Rose's avant-garde Tribeca salon, David Kleinberg's own dramatically sleek living room, and Jamie Drake's beautifully restored dining room in Gracie Mansion, the residence of the New York City mayor.

What makes a room magical?

Sometimes it's obvious: The gorgeous striped tenting of a foyer (Alex Papachristidis), the serene faux-granite walls of a penthouse sitting room (Stephen Sills), a jaw-dropping octagonal skylight in a double-height dining room (Sawyer | Berson).

Occasionally, the antiques and objets d'art are what make the room. As a former weekly antiques columnist for the *New York Times*, I was awestruck the first time I saw the seventeenth-century Italian *pietra dura* cabinet in the foyer of a collector's apartment on the Upper East Side. Festooned with rural scenes composed of bits of hard stone like lapis lazuli, malachite, and carnelian, the cabinet was made for the Medicis and spent many years in Buckingham Palace before the Windsors sold it at Christie's. I was equally smitten by Bunny Williams's mirrored canopy bed, a unique Serge Roche piece from the 1940s.

Some of the most inspirational rooms in this book are those that designers and artists created for themselves. The lovely, traditional Park Avenue bedroom that Mark Hampton created for himself and his wife, Duane, in the 1980s has barely changed for a good reason: it's perfect.

When the sculptor Donald Judd bought an entire cast-iron factory building in SoHo, he designated each floor by function (sleeping, working, entertaining). The "eating" floor is exceedingly spare: it has a long handmade wood table and set of chairs next to an open kitchen with a pot-bellied stove. The "decoration" is the amazing art, paintings and sculptures by his friends Frank Stella, John Chamberlain, Larry Bell, Dan Flavin, Lucas Samaras, and David Novros.

Similarly, the artist Julian Schnabel spent eight years designing, constructing, and decorating Palazzo Chupi, his elaborate Venetian-style apartment tower in Greenwich Village, which serves as his studio and residence (as well as home to some other fortunate residents).

New York is the epicenter of creativity in this country, and nowhere is that more evident than in the stunning private rooms shown here.

Wendy Moonan
New York, New York

Achille Salvagni Architetti

THE PURE TALENT of the young Roman architect Achille Salvagni is clearly evident in his first Manhattan project, a Fifth Avenue apartment overlooking Central Park.

His Long Island clients wanted a pied-à-terre where they could entertain. What he produced is a study in couture décor and the use of luxurious materials. He designed the silk-knotted rug and had it woven in Tibet. He created an octopus-like chandelier in gunmetal, patinated bronze, and onyx. He commissioned Miriam Ellner, one of the most sought-after glass artists, to create a unique verre églomisé mirror above the console he designed. He also created the drinks table, sconces, and candlesticks, which he had fabricated in workshops in Italy. The red pillows perfectly accent the prized, red Lucio Fontana painting that hangs above the fireplace.

Adolfo

ADOLFO F. SARDINA, the Cuban-born New York fashion designer known simply as Adolfo,
was a favorite of such society darlings as Jacqueline Onassis, C.Z. Guest, and Babe Paley.
He closed his salon in 1994 to focus on his licensing businesses, while he continued to live
very well in his elegant duplex in a nineteenth-century mansion on Fifth Avenue until 2014,
when he dispersed its contents. He and Edward C. Perry, his companion of forty years, had
filled it with Chinese and French antiques, Oriental carpets, and Old Master portraits from
France, Holland, Italy, and England. Adolfo once commented that he preferred portraits
over all other art: "I can talk to them," he said.

While the living room boasted baronial opulence, the cozy foyer was strictly organized, with
portraits and pairs (stone statues of Greek water carriers, wooden urns, antique sconces, and
rugs). Seventeenth-century portraits by Pieter Borselaer (top) and Pierre Mignard (bottom)
hung on the back of the cinnamon-red front door.

A HOUSE IN THE SKY
Aero Studios

WHEN DESIGNER THOMAS O'BRIEN moved to New York in 1979, it was to study photography, drawing, and painting—not architecture or design—at the Cooper Union. After graduating, he worked at the Ralph Lauren flagship store on Madison Avenue creating display vignettes on the home furnishings floor. This involved frequent trips to London and Paris to scour flea markets and antiques shops for props, often accompanied by Ralph Lauren himself. This may explain why he is as much a collector with a keen appreciation of fine vintage photography, antiquities, and American design classics, as he is an acclaimed interior designer.

In 1991, he founded Aero Studios. In 1997, he bought a luminous apartment on the seventeenth floor of the Parc Vendome condominium on West 57th Street because it had a twenty-foot-high living room ceiling with equally tall windows—his "house in the sky," as he calls it. "It's all about light and casement windows and symmetry," he adds. "It's so quintessentially New York." Here, he has amassed a stylish, carefully curated collection of works of art and furniture, including a massive George Nakashima Conoid dining table, two Harry Bertoia sound sculptures, a John Dickinson drinks table, and a vintage Eames chair. "It's mostly about American designers," O'Brien says of his collection of artworks and vintage furniture.

A prolific product designer himself, O'Brien created his ivory Deco Plaid rug as part of his line for Safavieh and the white Hallings secretary for Century Furniture. He also does fixtures for Circa Lighting, textile patterns for Lee Jofa, and barware, silver, and glassware for Reed & Barton.

Alex Papachristidis Interiors

NEW YORK DECORATOR Alex Papachristidis has warmth and charm and is greatly admired by his peers. (Mario Buatta famously once said, "If I weren't a decorator myself, I would hire him.")

Papachristidis comes from a very close family, so a few years ago, when a three-bedroom apartment became available in the Upper East Side building where his mother, nieces, and nephew were living, he jumped at the chance to join them. The apartment is in a modern building, however, so it presented challenges, particularly the low ceilings.

This was a limitation that inspired him, and the results are testimony to his talent. He tented the tiny foyer, covering the walls and mitered ceiling in a bold, turquoise striped fabric by Oscar de la Renta. "The fanciful tented foyer was inspired by the twentieth-century French decorator Georges Geffroy," says Papachristidis, referring to the legendary designer of houses, theater sets, and clothing who created Paris interiors for Daisy Fellowes and Gloria Guinness. "I always wanted [a tented space] like the one he designed for Arturo Lopez-Willshaw's yacht."

For his fantasy foyer, Papachristidis added a tole lantern with a garland of flowers, a whimsical dog sculpture, and an antique double-sided chinoiserie bookcase. It divides the space and, oddly enough, makes it seem larger. It's enchanting and, yes, you could be in Paris.

Alexander Gorlin Architects

IN 2008, New York architect Alexander Gorlin designed a library for a member of a prominent real estate family living in the heart of Manhattan. The client wanted a library that could also function as a cozy space for contemplation.

"My idea was to create a classic modern library with industrial touches that recalls, with its exposed structure, Henri Labrouste's beloved Bibliothèque nationale in Paris," Gorlin says. To this end, the architect invented a black steel and wood shelving system that would "combine the warmth of wood with the strength of steel."

Stenciling writers' names on the cornice is an explicit reference to Labrouste, who was widely criticized for carving the names of famous authors on the exterior of his other famous Parisian library, Sainte-Geneviève, in the 1840s. Gorlin's client selected the names of favorite authors to highlight in gold on the library's cornice, including the ancient Roman poet Virgil, author of the *Aeneid*, and Shakespeare. "His choice of Shakespeare, while not an uncommon choice, reflects his admiration for the bard's more obscure plays, like the tragedy *Titus Andronicus*," Gorlin says. The architect designed the mantel and fireplace surround with handmade, iridescent green Pewabic tiles from Detroit and installed the cherry floors. It is the owner's favorite room.

Billy Baldwin

IN THE 1960S, CBS studio head William S. Paley bought the ninth floor of 820 Fifth Avenue, a twelve-story Italian Renaissance–style palazzo that is still one of the city's most prestigious addresses.

Paley and his stylish wife, Babe, hired three firms to design their apartment: First, Maison Jansen of Paris installed eighteenth-century-style architectural paneling. Then, Parish-Hadley took over, rethinking the entire 6,500-square-foot space—except for the old sitting room. Finally, the owners looked to Billy Baldwin, the first man in New York to become an important decorator in a field dominated by women. The Paleys knew Baldwin well because he had designed their previous pied-à-terre in the St. Regis Hotel. They asked him to re-create the library from their place from the St. Regis at 820 Fifth, and the dapper decorator covered the walls with a printed brown Indian cotton gathered in pleats, like a tent. Mrs. Paley contributed the blackamoor-bordered needlepoint carpet and the strikingly original chandelier, a Moorish blackamoor perched on a clock.

Baldwin did many grand schemes for blue bloods, including Jacqueline Onassis, Nan Kempner, and Bunny Mellon. The Paley library décor is suitably charming and quiet, the perfect background for the family's outstanding collection of antique French gilt bronzes and Post-Impressionist paintings.

Bradfield & Tobin

RENOWNED FOR THE GLAMOROUS apartments he has created for his A-list clients all over the world, New York interior designer Geoffrey Bradfield has created a series of homes for himself that rival even those of his clients. One of his favorites was his penultimate: an East Side Manhattan town house, built in 1869, which he transformed in 2006 into a fantasy of white-on-white rooms.

Here, the scene-stealer was the reception room, which opened into a garden courtyard. It had twelve white Ionic columns, which were up-lit from the floor. Between many of the columns were full-length panels of mirror and white plaster sconces. Bradfield furnished the room with a clear acrylic neoclassical round table and Klismos chairs (from his Millennium Modern collection) that seem to disappear in the space. This foyer is like a dream.

Brian J. McCarthy, Inc.

TWENTY YEARS AGO, when a bachelor investment banker had the opportunity to buy another floor in his prewar Sutton Place building, he jumped at the chance. The apartment had already been gutted by the seller—not a ceiling, wall, or floor was left—so he had a clean slate.

He asked New York classical architect Boris Baranovich and New York interior designer Brian J. McCarthy to collaborate in rethinking and rebuilding the space from the ground up. The traditional entrance hall is very grand and has an Old World feeling, but everything is brand new and custom designed for the space, from the geometric Cotswold limestone floor to the faux-marble Ionic columns, carved classical moldings, and mahogany doors. Only the dolphin-base table and light fixtures are old, both nineteenth-century antiques from France. McCarthy is famously versatile in his practice; he may live with modern things at home but he is equally capable of producing grand traditional spaces with classical proportions and an Old World sensibility, as he has done here.

Brian J. McCarthy, Inc.

THE LATE INVESTMENT BANKER Christopher H. Brown, a longtime client of New York decorator Brian J. McCarthy, wanted his Sutton Place dining room to look as English as possible, with Chippendale chairs, an Adam sideboard, a Wedgwood glass chandelier, and lots of good eighteenth-century English silver. But when it came to the wall mural, he told McCarthy that he wanted to commission an American landscape, not an English one, even though he wanted it to be painted in the style of an English eighteenth-century landscape picture.

McCarthy went to the upstate New York decorative artist Susan Huggins, and her expansive painting of the Hudson River Valley, which covers all four walls, produces a dreamy atmospheric backdrop for the room's fine English antiques and Sultanabad carpet.

Bunny Willliams

IN 2010, New York master designer Bunny Williams created a showstopping dining room for a client on Park Avenue and 72nd Street. "[It's] all about drama," Williams says. First she carved niches into the walls to showcase the client's antique busts of the Four Seasons. Then she upholstered the walls in brown silk taffeta to serve as a background for the contemporary paintings, a stunning Allegra Hicks carpet, and a set of fine Regency dining chairs.

The focal point is a sunburst mirror that Williams designed after seeing something similar above a William Kent fireplace in Badminton, England. She had it made by Miriam Ellner, a world-renowned New York glass artist who specializes in verre églomisé, the art of gilding metals on the reverse side of glass. The mirror hangs above an elegant proto-modern fireplace modeled after one that the neoclassical architect Sir John Soane created in the early 1800s for a house in England. Williams designed the dining table, inspired by a table that Maison Jansen made for the Duchess of Windsor, with faux bamboo bronze legs secured by golden cords. The room is opulent and modern.

AN ENCHANTING REFUGE
Bunny Williams

AFTER THIRTY YEARS of running her own business, Bunny Williams has become an expert at producing stylish, comfortable, grand bedrooms, partly because she thinks they are crucial refuges in a busy world. The bedroom she shares with her husband, antiques dealer John Rosselli, is also a sitting room. "I spend about two hours in bed before I go to work," Williams says. "I spread out my newspapers and books and magazines, make phone calls, watch the news, have breakfast on a tray. It's *my* time."

And with its canopy covered in mirrored tiles, what a dazzling bed she has! It is a Serge Roche design from the 1940s that Rosselli spotted at a sleepy auction preview. "It was a pile of mirrors on the floor," he recalls. "But I had a hunch—it had belonged to [the philanthropist] Dorothy Hart Hirshon, Bill Paley's first wife—so I bought it for Bunny." Williams adds, "What's so beautiful is the way every piece is beveled, tapered—almost like jewels." Williams commissioned Lesage in Paris to do the silk embroidery for the headboard. "I was inspired by an antique piece of appliquéd satin I had; it could have been from Syria or Morocco," she says.

The bedroom walls are lined with a platinum tea paper from Gracie. The valance over the window is covered in a striped Turkish silk with a glass-bead fringe. Atop the painted antique English dressing table is an antique mirror with a silver repoussé frame, which Williams thinks is from Spain. The white column-form lamps are from the 1940s, sourced from John Rosselli Antiques.

Cabinet Alberto Pinto

THE LATE CELEBRATED Paris decorator Alberto Pinto, whose sister now runs the eponymous firm, for decades worked all over the world with some of the richest clients on earth. In the 1980s, in particular, he designed several opulent interiors in Manhattan, including this foyer in a large, seven-story mansion on the Upper East Side.

His client, a New York art collector, had particularly eclectic taste, so Pinto's challenge was to combine harmoniously, in a soaring stair hall, a large Roman marble Hercules, a Hollywood movie spotlight, ancient Syrian mosaics, and a fine eighteenth-century French sofa signed by Charles Cressent, cabinetmaker to the king of France. It is a dramatic success.

Cabinet Alberto Pinto

COLLECTORS AROUND THE WORLD—Kuwait, Morocco, New York, London, Cairo, and Courchevel—have long been attracted to the Alberto Pinto office in Paris, because the design team is so masterful at incorporating art and antiques into the décor of private residences. In one overscaled nineteenth-century town house on Fifth Avenue where he worked in 2008, Pinto guaranteed that his client's guests would be impressed as they approached the rotunda antechamber of the dining room from the monumental entrance.

Before passing through the threshold into the antechamber, guests would experience a bit of stagecraft: a wall dotted with brackets displaying dozens of pieces of antique Chinese blue-and-white porcelain, beautifully arranged between the lintel and the monumentally tall ceiling. The porcelains were acquired in the auction of pieces recovered from the so-called Ca Mau shipwreck. In 1998, some Vietnamese fisherman trawling in the Ca Mau peninsula in southern Vietnam caught their nets in the wreck of an eighteenth-century Chinese junk. Evidently, there had been a fire on board and the ship sank en route from China to Jakarta. The porcelains, which came from kilns all over China, had been made for the export market; many displayed European motifs. The dishes could be accurately dated because they bore the mark of Emperor Yongzheng, who reigned during the Qing dynasty from 1723 to 1735. This is how a great designer incorporates works of art to their best effect in a domestic setting.

THE ART OF THE INVISIBLE

Cabinet Alberto Pinto

WHEN A COUPLE purchased a three-story apartment in a town house on Fifth Avenue overlooking Central Park, they gained a palatial living room in eighteenth-century French style that had been created in 1885 by the Parisian firm Jules Allard et Fils. Remarkably, the lacy ornamental plasterwork on the salon ceiling had been left in place, so the family's designer, the fantasist Alberto Pinto, gave it a thorough restoration and then lightened the look by contrasting the white plaster with Wedgwood-blue walls.

Pinto accompanied the couple while they collected French antiques and Old Master paintings in Paris, which he then incorporated into the scheme. He also added whimsical elements like the fantasy gilt-wood chair with seahorse armrests and the herringbone book cabinet. "The paradox of great interior design is that it is the art of the invisible, of choreographing the spaces between things to make them sing," Pinto's friend, the British artist Marc Quinn writes about the designer's oeuvre. "Alberto is the master of this invisible art."

GRAND TOUR FANTASY
Calhoun Sumrall

CALHOUN SUMRALL, a fashion designer who formerly headed the Lauren division of Ralph Lauren, is also a dreamer. When he arrived in New York from Louisiana twenty-seven years ago, he was lucky enough to find a small, extremely affordable apartment in a Greenwich Village town house, which he furnished with finds from neighborhood antiques shops and local flea markets. He soon became friendly with his elderly landlords, Dr. Henriette Stoner and her husband, Elmer Cecil Stoner, an artist who had been involved with the Harlem Renaissance. They lived in a duplex penthouse that had been added to the building after the Second World War. After they passed away, Sumrall moved into their space, which had been designed in the California Mission Revival style, with wrought-iron railings and chandeliers, massive skylights, colorful tiles, and a Juliet balcony. "With the twenty-six-foot-tall ceiling, I imagined I was a bohemian living on the French Riviera or the Bay of Naples," the designer recalls.

Eventually, Sumrall met the English interior designer Robert Kime (whose clients include Prince Charles) and the antiques dealer Michael Trapp, both of whom became mentors. With their help, he created a nineteenth-century-style interior that became his Grand Tour fantasy. "I kept falling in love with older and older things," he says. He bought eighteenth-century Swedish and French armchairs, a Swedish sofa, a pair of nineteenth-century faux-bamboo Regency chairs, and, at the Grand Bazaar in Istanbul, five antique Persian *soumak* carpets. He added antique Italian vases, wall-mounted water buffalo horns, and a drawing by Jean Cocteau. "I always need a creative process," says Sumrall, who is currently rescuing a house in New Orleans. His former apartment is testimony to the creative process of a true dreamer.

SOUTHERN HOSPITALITY ON THE UPPER EAST SIDE

Charlotte Moss

BORN IN RICHMOND, Virginia, Charlotte Moss has charm, humor, incredible energy, and a surfeit of talents. Moss—whose mantles include those of interior designer; author; gardener; activist; designer of fabrics, furniture, and china; and philanthropist—has a simple decorating mantra: "I'm interested in creating places that make you and your guests comfortable." The guest bedroom in her own Upper East Side town house certainly follows this ideology.

The room is an ode to chinoiserie, with a matching pair of ebonized, antique English four-poster beds, a green chinoiserie dressing table, an antique chinoiserie desk, and a chinoiserie mirror above the fireplace. The raspberry-hued peony print on the beds and walls is vintage Manuel Canovas. Moss had saved a sample from decades ago. When she found the pattern had been discontinued, she persuaded Canovas to revive it just for her. Ever the gracious hostess, she installed a hidden kitchen in the bedroom where guests can prepare breakfast—or have a nightcap—on their own. The room is a perfect embodiment of her Southern hospitality.

Cullman & Kravis Associates

VETERAN NEW YORK DECORATOR Ellie Cullman is renowned for the comfort and style of her bedrooms. When a longtime client asked for an update for her large Park Avenue apartment on the Upper East Side without a full renovation—"with four children and three dogs, they weren't about to relocate"—Cullman managed it.

In the master bedroom, she went for luxe. She had the walls upholstered in a pale cream ottoman silk and finished with bronze nail heads. The bronze tones are repeated in the metallic threads of the Lesage-embroidered cuffs on the silk curtains, the mirror frames, the chandelier, the gold leather chairs, the monogrammed linens, and the custom bedside tables. Such attention to detail is truly remarkable but typical of Cullman's signature style.

TAILORED LUXURY

Darren Henault Interiors

NEW YORK DECORATOR Darren Henault is widely admired for creating layered interiors that blend Old World charm with modern comfort. (He calls his style "luxurious, tailored and traditional.") At home, Henault, his husband, and their two daughters have lived in a duplex maisonette for eight years. It is on the ground floor of a grand limestone and redbrick Georgian mansion on Fifth Avenue that was built in 1896 by the coal magnate Edward J. Berwind. The then-largest supplier of bituminous coal in the country (including to the U.S. Navy), Berwind and his wife hired the prestigious Paris decorating firm Jules Allard et Fils to create a palace-like interior, complete with a Louis XV–style ballroom. Berwind died in 1942 and, amazingly, his original interiors have not been altered in some of the rooms. Henault's living room is the former library, with the original painted ceiling and mahogany paneling embellished with bronze ormolu mounts.

Henault likes antiques and knows how to incorporate them seamlessly into his interiors. Here, he has decorated the room for entertaining—he is a wonderful host—with comfortable vintage André Arbus armchairs, a vintage modern T. H. Robsjohn-Gibbings daybed, Charles X side tables, and a white goatskin coffee table that he designed for the space. Huge passementerie tassels on the elaborately layered curtains complement the fringed lampshades. Henault knows just where and how to splurge for maximum impact.

EXQUISITE PROPORTIONS

David Kleinberg
Design Associates

NEW YORK DESIGNER David Kleinberg seemed destined to buy his twelfth-floor floor-through apartment on East 72nd Street. He had known about the residence since 1983, when Denning & Fourcade published it. (Kleinberg would later work for that firm, which is known for its opulent, Old World interiors.) Back then, the walls were faux bois with green silk damask panels, and the ceiling was wallpapered. But what had struck Kleinberg most of all were the European proportions—it was almost a perfect double cube, with floor-to-ceiling casement windows. "The apartment had belonged to George Gershwin in the 1930s," Kleinberg says, "and I was lucky to inherit a lot of the [original] architecture— in all the years it had changed hands, people had not touched it."

To enhance the classical details, Kleinberg painted the walls chalk white, then waxed and buffed the paneling. He inserted round mirrors in the openings above the sconces and added a pale braided sisal rug and white cut-velvet club chairs. For contrast, he designed the elegant black lacquer cabinet with its gilded stand, after spotting a similar French midcentury model at an auction. The cabinet, a cane-backed, early twentieth-century Swedish chair, and a dark contemporary painting by Garth Weiser pop out against the luminous background. The pièce de résistance is the early twentieth-century Swedish light fixture. "It came out of a banqueting hall, and I love its swirly, curly gilded-wood armature," Kleinberg says. "I wish I could find the others from that room."

David Kleinberg Design Associates

IN 2009, when a couple, both serious art collectors, bought an adjoining apartment in their Park Avenue building, they asked New York designer David Kleinberg to reconfigure the combined eight-thousand-square-foot space.

This two-year project gave Kleinberg the latitude to create a large new kitchen with Calacatta marble counters and backsplashes, Poul Henningsen pendant light fixtures, and custom stainless-steel and milk-glass cabinets (the couple has three children, and they love to entertain). The wife, who is from Southern California, loves bright colors, which may explain her attraction to the enormous round painting by Takashi Murakami in the breakfast room.

Kleinberg is a modernist who runs his office in a modern way. He recently granted his five most senior designers equity partnerships in the firm, which is quite rare in the design business. He realized how much his team enjoyed working together, so he devised a plan to create an environment that would keep them there, thus positioning the firm, now DKDA, for the future. It is just the opposite of what happened at Parish-Hadley, where Kleinberg spent sixteen years. One by one, his colleagues at the firm left to open their own offices, as did he. Parish-Hadley closed after Albert Hadley's death.

THE MEDICAL BIBLIOPHILE
David Ling Architect

MOST SERIOUS BOOK COLLECTORS have old-fashioned libraries with wooden bookshelves lining the walls, but not this Manhattan neurosurgeon, who has amassed four thousand rare fifteenth- through eighteenth-century medical texts over the past four decades.

The doctor and his wife did something quite radical after they became empty nesters: instead of moving to a smaller place, they kept their high-floor, three-bedroom apartment on the Upper East Side, not wanting to give up their wonderful city views. To rethink the space, they looked to David Ling, a Manhattan modernist who had a radical idea: he suggested gutting the apartment and reconfiguring it to highlight the rare book collection.

For the library, the centerpiece of the apartment, he designed custom sandblasted glass shelves supported by ebonized black-oak panels. The glass shelves are backlit so they glow at night. They are also deep enough to accommodate a double row of volumes, because "books are like rabbits," the doctor jokes. "You put them on shelves and they multiply." Ling laid new, white-maple floors and replaced the windows with UV-filter glass to safeguard the books and the works of art. He also dropped the ceiling to create a cove for both indirect and track lighting.

Ling then furnished the library with a seventeenth-century refectory table, good for laying out books to study, and modern pieces—a loveseat and sling-back chairs by Le Corbusier and a Ludwig Mies van der Rohe Barcelona table—that float above a colorful antique carpet. "It's a dialogue between new and old," the doctor says. And does he continue to buy books? "Hourly," he replies with a smile.

David Monn, LLC and Gwathmey Siegel Kaufman Architects

WHILE MOST NEW YORKERS know David Monn as one of the city's most exclusive event planners, he is also an accomplished interior designer. In 2005, *Esquire* asked him to create a billiards room in an "Ultimate Bachelor Pad," a show house the magazine was sponsoring with The Related Companies, a privately owned real estate company. Related had commissioned the architect Charles Gwathmey to design the twenty-one-story residential condominium, now known as Astor Place Tower.

Monn was given a twenty-seven-by-eighteen-foot space with distinctive curvilinear floor-to-ceiling windows. Inspired by the 1960s, Monn decided to turn it into a "mod" room with a white, gray, and silver palette. He covered the floor in white patent leather and added a white sheepskin rug and white upholstered furniture. The custom Blatt Billiards table is made of polished chrome and boasts a steel-gray suede top instead of the traditional green. All of the pool balls except the cue ball (which is red) are black and white.

Monn designed the light fixture above the table with shimmering crystal rods. Additional lighting comes from a pair of vintage floor lamps with chrome shades. The producers of Maker's Mark bourbon oversaw the making of the red-wax-covered bar. It is the same wax that is used to seal the distillery's liquor bottles and in the same signature color. This glamorous, sophisticated décor particularly comes alive at night, with uninterrupted views of the Empire State Building and the Met Life Tower.

David Scott Parker Architects

BASED IN SOUTHPORT, Connecticut, David Scott Parker is a rare combination of architect and antiques dealer. He is also acclaimed for his meticulous preservation work, notably at the United States Treasury in Washington, D.C., and the Williamsburg Savings Bank in Brooklyn.

In 1999, a young New York couple asked Parker to restore a five-story 1880s brownstone on the Upper East Side. All that was left of its original interior were the doorframes and woodwork, and they asked him to return it to its 1880s splendor. Parker began acquiring period metalwork, furniture, wallpaper, lighting, fireplaces, textiles, and other pieces of decorative art. Because he specializes in the Aesthetic Movement as a dealer, he was able to supply some of the antiques himself, but he also went to such experts as interiors historian Mimi Findlay for advice in locating Tiffany stained glass, Herter Brothers chairs, William Morris fabrics, and Théodore Deck faience planters. He found wainscoting from a former Theodore Roosevelt house and cabinets that had been originally made for Chateau-sur-Mer, a mansion in Newport, Rhode Island. It took many years to finish, but this project is a remarkable accomplishment; the entire family loves it and uses every single room.

David Scott Parker Architects

THE CHALLENGE IN RESTORING and rebuilding an 1882 Manhattan brownstone is for it to be fully modernized without looking that way. Architect David Scott Parker is a master of this craft. In fact, this particular project has been recognized by the New York Landmarks Conservancy with a Lucy G. Moses preservation award and by the Institute of Classical Architecture and Art with a Stanford White award. For a couple and their children in the only one-family brownstone left on their block on East 72nd Street, Parker had the house updated with a new HVAC system and smart-house technology.

Parker designed the new kitchen on the top floor next to the family room, so food could be prepared in natural light from the period clear-glass laylights in the ceiling. Parker designed the island, cabinetry, and door surround that his team of ace woodcarvers beautifully realized, adding delicately incised and stained floral flourishes. The band of acanthus leaves on the lintel is a particular tour de force of craftsmanship.

David Scott Parker Architects

"IT WAS A JOY," says architect David Scott Parker, describing his decade-long restoration and decoration of a five-story brownstone on East 72nd Street. Parker says his clients, serious aficionados of the Aesthetic Movement, "asked me to make the house look as if it was newly completed, to show the vitality and brightness it would have had in 1880."

The master bathroom, however, is brand new. For it, Parker commissioned two skilled New York carvers to do the overmantel and cabinetry in maple because, he explains, "1880 was just the moment when woodwork was becoming lighter." The room has a nature theme. The kingfisher cornice is a reproduction of a period wallpaper. He specified starlings for the wallpaper on the ceiling and butterflies for the paper borders. The bathtub is carved out of a single piece of Thassos snow-white marble. The cut-crystal chandelier is from the 1880s by Thackera, Sons and Company. Christopher Dresser designed the turquoise majolica amphora on the wood stand as an exhibition piece for Minton. The faux-bamboo dressing table is by R. J. Horner & Co. of New York. Parker designed the upper sash of the window; the lower is original, with Tiffany clear-glass tiles.

Deborah Berke Partners

BRIEFLY REIGNING as the tallest residential tower in the Western Hemisphere, New York–based architect Rafael Viñoly's 432 Park is notable not only for its ninety-six stories but also for its exposed exoskeleton. Each apartment has ten-foot-square windows and twelve-and-a-half-foot ceilings, so the rooms have astounding views of the city and surrounding geography.

New York architect and dean of the Yale School of Architecture Deborah Berke was commissioned to design the interiors, and the kitchens and bathrooms particularly reflect her minimalist style. Each master bathroom has statuary book-matched white marble walls and radiant-heated floors, with a freestanding soaking tub placed right next to the window. The twelve-hundred-pound vanity is solid Bianco Sivec marble with custom counter cabinets and medicine chest. Berke's design for the bathroom is luxurious but also quite plain; in her interiors for this building Berke wisely decided not to compete with, but to embrace, the breathtaking views.

Denning & Fourcade

THE LATE OSCAR DE LA RENTA and his widow, Annette, have long been celebrated for their creativity, their art, their personal styles, their smashing dinner parties—and their jaw-dropping Park Avenue apartment. When they bought the apartment in the 1980s, they went to Denning & Fourcade, at the time New York's favorite purveyors of staggering opulence, to create a luxurious background for their art and antiques. Almost singlehandedly, Robert Denning and Vincent Fourcade are credited with reintroducing the sumptuous nineteenth-century French Second Empire style to Manhattan, to high-profile clients like New York financier Henry Kravis and French banker Michel David-Weill.

For de la Renta, the suave Dominican-American couturier, the team provided a Rothschild-style living room where he could hold court from cocktail hour to long after dinner. The dominant color is red: garnet curtains, a stately double sofa (a signature Fourcade design), a bench covered in crimson needlepoint, and a Napoleon III carpet loomed to look as if it were Turkish. (Fourcade once said that a room without a touch of red was "like a woman without lipstick.") Into this mix they added a Boulle-style black-lacquered cabinet; a series of pictures, including an Egyptian landscape by Eugène Fromentin; bronze busts; and sculptures.

As Fourcade once explained, "Outrageous luxury is what our clients want." And that is precisely what they got.

Donald Judd

IN 1968, artist Donald Judd purchased a five-story cast-iron building at 101 Spring Street in SoHo. Built in 1870, the former garment factory was not in good shape but the floor plates were huge—twenty-five by seventy-five feet—and the façades were mostly glass windows, so the interiors were flooded with daylight. Judd decided to renovate it and turn it into his house, studio, and gallery.

"It was pretty certain that each floor had been open, since there were no signs of original walls, which determined that each floor should have one purpose: sleeping, eating, working," Judd wrote in a 1989 essay about the loft. And that is what he did. The floor for eating includes a large open kitchen—its shelves still full of Judd's earthenware plates and pots and pans—with a cast-iron pot-bellied stove and a dining area with minimalist handcrafted furniture and walls displaying art. "I spent a great deal of time placing the art and a great deal designing the renovation in accordance," he continues. "Everything from the first was intended to be thoroughly considered and to be permanent."

After Judd's death in 1994, his children formed the Judd Foundation, which meticulously restored the building as a museum, now open by appointment. Today, it looks as if the family is still in residence, with Judd's furniture and many of his own works of art complemented by those of his friends Frank Stella, Dan Flavin, John Chamberlain, Sol LeWitt, Philip Guston, and Clyfford Still. At the time of this photograph, the David Novros mural (shown at left) appears in a damaged state. It has since been restored by the foundation.

Doug Meyer Studio

DOUG MEYER IS A MAN of many talents: artist, interior decorator, textile designer, art and antiques collector, and author. In 2012, a couple asked him to design their duplex in a what was then a brand-new luxury apartment building by architect Annabelle Selldorf on West 22nd Street and Eleventh Avenue. (It may be the only building in the city where you can drive your car into an elevator and park it right outside your apartment.) "Even though the wife is British, [the couple] gravitate toward American art," Meyer says. "They collect American art photography, and the husband has a fascination with flags, so my idea was to do the whole place in red, white, and blue. That's why the living room is red and the bedroom is blue."

The living room walls are white, to best display pictures (by Diane Arbus, Robert Mapplethorpe, Robert Capa, and Andy Warhol). Meyer designed the red rug based on what he calls the "circle drip pieces" that he had already painted on Plexiglas panels in the entry. As he explains, "So the red rug becomes this island of red and everything on it is red, as if growing out of the rug." That includes the vintage Warren Platner chairs, the Dunbar armless low chairs, and the vintage Jens Risom sofa—all upholstered in red textiles (wool, felt, velvet, or suede). Meyer even designed a small table with neon stripes for the room. When viewed from the second-floor landing, the décor is especially dazzling. "For me, these projects are very much a site-specific installation," Meyer says. "And, happily, my clients view the apartment as a work of art in and of itself. The only thing that changes is the art on the walls."

Fairfax & Sammons Architects

IN 1996, Donald Oresman, a retired corporate lawyer and philanthropist, went to Richard Sammons to create a library for his pied-à-terre on Central Park South. The library was to house his extensive collection of books of literary criticism, fiction, and poetry, and eighteen hundred works of art, each one depicting a person or people in the act of reading. Quite suitably, the pied-à-terre was located in Gainsborough Studios, a 1905 building that Charles W. Buckham designed for artists with studios that had north-facing windows.

Oresman's brief to Sammons: transform the narrow, double-height former artist's studio into a Renaissance-style library that could provide maximum storage for the books as well as properly display his art. He also wanted to add a perch from which he could watch birds flying in Central Park.

Sammons designed fitted-out bookcases of pale polished maple that project at right angles into the room from the sidewalls in a series of bays beneath the deeply coffered ceiling. Each surface is articulated with classical details, with moldings and pediments carefully added. Mezzanine galleries boast more shelving and provide access to a sleeping balcony. Sammons says the graceful spiral staircase was inspired by one in the Loretto Chapel in Santa Fe, New Mexico.

The library doubles as a living room, with deep sofas in the center and a dining area behind. Beyond the dining room is a small kitchen, bathroom, and sitting room. About three hundred works of art are displayed throughout the space, some hanging on hinged panels that open out from the wall. Others are affixed to sliding panels or in custom portfolio drawers tucked under the stairs.

Gabellini Sheppard Associates

THE CORE OF THIS thirty-five-hundred-square-foot penthouse on Park Avenue is a spare living room designed to showcase the owner's important collection of vintage and contemporary photographs.

New York architect Michael Gabellini is a master of the minimalist interior. Here, he has created a graphic composition of white, black, and gray walls that respond to the natural light pouring in from the terrace. The black-stained mahogany wall is perfect for displaying images while hiding interior storage. The white French plaster walls boast ever-changing exhibitions of the couple's rare photographs. Built into the ceiling reveals, the unique art-hanging system is almost invisible. The custom-designed, satin-finish stainless-steel coffee table, Yoshiro Taniguchi lounge chairs, and Giovanni Alfredi velvet sofa float above a beige Spanish limestone floor. This is a room for the contemplation of art.

NATURE AND WHIMSY
Gabellini Sheppard Associates

IN 2007, after a young professional couple bought a 1920s industrial loft adjacent to the High Line in Chelsea, they asked their New York architecture firm, Gabellini Sheppard, to reconfigure the four-thousand-square-foot space as both art gallery and residence. The dining area, with white plaster walls and a naturally tinted poured-concrete floor, has a massive wood table that can seat ten, which was commissioned from Miya Shoji, a furniture store/workshop on West 18th Street. This table—by venerable Japanese master craftsman Hisao Hanafusa and his son Zui—is made of bubinga, a fine-grained African wood. The chairs in walnut and woven grass were custom ordered from the George Nakashima workshop in New Hope, Pennsylvania.

Hovering above the table is a special commission in the Blossom chandelier series fabricated by Dutch design star Tord Boontje, who said this particular one was inspired by a blossoming branch of a fruit tree after an ice storm. The architects selected different Swarovski crystals that were assembled in flowerlike clusters and then attached by hand to an armature festooned with LED lights. The crystals glow, sparkle, reflect, and deflect light, giving the room a sculptural, whimsical sensibility.

Gabellini Sheppard Associates

IN 2015, two years after Gabellini Sheppard finished a top-to-bottom, seven-year reconstruction of a handsome Warren & Wetmore town house on the Upper East Side for a young couple with four children, the clients returned to the firm with a new request: they wanted an indoor swimming pool.

The complicated project required excavating thirty feet below the house—no mean engineering feat—to add two subterranean levels to the five stories above ground. After installing a light well in the garden, the firm was able to illuminate the pool with both natural and artificial cove lighting. The pool is surrounded by white marble, giving it a luminous glow "almost like a grotto," suggests Michael Gabellini. It is also a space for contemplation, not just swimming.

Gabellini Sheppard Associates

FOR A COUPLE in the world of fashion who bought a thirty-five-hundred-square-foot penthouse on Park Avenue, Gabellini Sheppard designed a unique, minimalist bathroom in the corner of the master bedroom.

Finished in fine-grained, honed Bianco Sivec marble, the bathroom visually expands the volume of the bedroom. Its custom-made marble sink is designed like a miniature gravity pool, and the bathtub—also marble—is carved from a single, immense block of the same stone. Two walls are composed of sliding glass panels that change from transparent to translucent at the flip of a switch, allowing privacy. The adjoining bedroom is much larger than it appears. The black ribbon mahogany headboard is actually a wall that separates the sleeping area from a large walk-in wardrobe. The bed, which appears to be floating above the honed Spanish limestone floor, is made of pale anigre, an African hardwood. Each side of the bed has a pull-out console to control sound, lighting, temperature, and the solar shades. The suite of rooms represents the height of refined luxury.

Gabellini Sheppard Associates

GABELLINI SHEPPARD ASSOCIATES used to be known for the minimalist boutiques it created in Paris, Rome, London, and Beijing for such high-end retailers as Giorgio Armani, Jil Sander, and Salvatore Ferragamo. In fact, it was the conversion of a nineteenth-century Paris building to a sleek Sander emporium that caught the eye of a young New York couple. In 2006, they had just bought a handsome five-story Beaux-Arts limestone Upper East Side house, built by Warren & Wetmore in 1903.

The couple asked the firm to convert the nine-unit apartment house to a one-family home, a process that took seven years. "We took the back wall off and rebuilt it," Michael Gabellini recalls. Then, two years after it was done, the clients returned with a new program: they wanted a swimming pool, gym, and basketball half-court under the house. This required major excavation, but the basketball court doesn't feel as if it's underground. Gabellini Sheppard put a light well into the garden that allows natural light to penetrate the space below. Then they added cove lighting to the fixtures in the ceiling, so the court can be used night or day.

Gachot Studios

DAVID KARP, the thirty-something founder and former chief executive officer of Tumblr, owns a duplex loft in the Williamsburg neighborhood of Brooklyn. It is a quiet, understated space with exposed brick walls, reclaimed oak floors, and tin ceilings—in addition to sweeping views of Manhattan across the East River. In his renovation of the space, Karp worked with John Gachot, cofounder with his wife, Christine, of Gachot Studios, a New York firm best known for its hotel and spa designs. Gachot helped source the vintage materials and midcentury furniture that Karp likes, including a pair of Poul Kjaerholm leather chairs, a Niels Bendtsen sofa, and an Eero Saarinen–designed chair for Knoll. He also devised ways to display Karp's beloved 1959 Honda motorcycle and his collections of old cameras and classic board games. There is no pretension to this interior. The open kitchen features soapstone countertops, and the upstairs bedroom has steel and glass walls. One of Karp's favorite areas accommodates a classic claw-foot bathtub (the rest of the master bathroom is down the hall), which overlooks the living room and affords views of the city beyond.

Such a pared-down, basic interior may seem surprising for a high-tech web developer, until one recalls that simplicity is part of Tumblr's DNA—it was designed to make it easy to start a blog and begin posting within minutes. Here, in a similar way, form does follow function.

Georgis & Mirgorodsky

IN 2001, the ultra-talented New York architect William T. Georgis utterly transformed a five-story Upper East Side town house, which had been built in 1910. He reconfigured the entire building as a single-family residence for himself along with professional offices for his firm. He installed a new glass curtain wall in the rear of the house, which afforded him a double-height living room with a garden view. He has filled the premises with important contemporary art sourced by his late partner, Richard D. Marshall, including paintings by Julian Schnabel and Christopher Wool, and sculptures by Scott Burton and Lynda Benglis.

The décor is whimsical and wildly eclectic. Contemporary works of art hang over Baroque antiques and under a vintage disco ball. Georgis designed the silk-velvet zebra slipper chairs. An ancient Roman torso shares space with an Alex Katz portrait of Georgis, which is reflected in the mirrored screen in front of the black marble fireplace. "The important thing was to create a vibrant, unorthodox mix that surprises and creates both visual and ideological juxtapositions," Georgis says.

Giovannini Design Associates

NEW YORK– AND LOS ANGELES–BASED architect Joseph Giovannini may be best known as an architecture critic and author, but he has designed apartments and lofts that are the equal to the buildings he has reviewed. Although he coined the term Deconstructivism in 1987, in 2015 he resolved to keep things simple for his own sixteen-hundred-square-foot apartment in Murray Hill, creating an architecture of light functioning as a canvas for a three-dimensional tribute to Mondrian.

"I couldn't afford Mondrian's *Broadway Boogie Woogie*, so I built it," he says, referring to the famous 1942–43 painting composed of horizontal and vertical blocks of red, blue, yellow, black, and white. Working in the tight dimensions of an Art Deco apartment built during the Great Depression, he played off the exposed beams and columns, transforming them into wands of indirect light whose glow dissolves walls and expands dimensions. Within the luminous rooms, he painted space by projecting blocks of red, blue, and green across surfaces, so that they detach, appearing to float. The color blocks slip in and out of register as the eye moves through the apartment, forming a kinetic illusion.

Gloria Vanderbilt

"COLOR IS TO THE EYE what music is to the ear," American artist and designer Louis Comfort Tiffany wrote in *The Art Work of Louis C. Tiffany* in 1914. He could have easily been describing the unique palette of Gloria Vanderbilt, the socialite, author, artist, and founder of a blue jeans empire. She is also a talented decorator, as proven by the patchwork-quilt bedroom she once designed for herself in an Upper East Side town house.

The inspiration for it came by accident. As Ms. Vanderbilt recalls, she and her late husband Wyatt were strolling down Main Street in Southampton, New York, one afternoon when they saw a store that sold nothing but antique American patchwork quilts. "We just went in and started collecting them," she says. The couturier Adolfo, learning of her new passion, later designed a dress for her, inspired by the rich colors and pieced-together artistry of the craft. "From that came the idea to do a room," she says. "I put them all over and found my paintings worked well on walls of quilts."

Though lost after Ms. Vanderbilt moved house, the room is still legendary in the world of interior decoration.

109

GLUCK+

AS PART OF the larger design of a modern thirteen-bedroom town house in Borough Park, Brooklyn, veteran New York architect Peter L. Gluck, of the Harlem-based firm GLUCK+, designed the foyer to separate the public and private domains of the residence (the husband regularly hosts study groups in the library and doesn't want the meetings to disturb his large family).

The sliding glass-paneled doors in the foyer separate the entry from the sky-lit stair hall, while, behind the bench, glazed, louvered panels purposefully obscure the stairs and those using them. The spaces are unified by the quiet palette of off-white limestone flooring, etched glass, and natural wood.

OLD WORLD CHARM

Helen Fioratti

HELEN FIORATTI IS BEST KNOWN as the owner of the enchanting Upper East Side gallery L'Antiquaire & The Connoisseur. Her mother, Countess Ruth Costantino, who is thought to be the first female fine art dealer in America, ran it before her. The gallery offers a wide array of European decorative arts and antiques, from ancient Byzantine mosaics to eighteenth-century French and Italian furniture and Old Master drawings. Fioratti has also written several books on the decorative arts in both Italian and English.

What is less known about Fioratti is that she is an accomplished decorator who has been designing residences all over the world, particularly in the Middle East, for decades. For a collector on the Upper East Side, Fioratti created an Old World setting for the owner's collection of Renaissance art, including fifteenth-century Italian paintings of the saints, sixteenth-century French lion's-head chairs, an antique Oushak rug from Turkey, and, on the mantel, a pair of Flemish Gothic candlesticks from the 1500s. The walls and ceiling panels are covered in golden velvet. The faux-marble pilasters and beams were painted "to best complement the art," Fioratti explains. Among the other delightful treasures is a magnificent Italian Renaissance *pietra dura* cabinet-on-stand in the entrance hall.

Henri Samuel

THERE ARE FEW winter gardens in New York City, and the most unforgettable is located in one of the finest apartment buildings in town: the 1931 twelve-story limestone-clad co-op at 834 Fifth Avenue. Among the many duplexes in the building is a twelve-thousand-square-foot apartment that the late John Gutfreund and his wife, Susan, bought in 1984.

Mrs. Gutfreund, a Francophile, is an avid decorator and antiques collector. She had already purchased a set of eighteenth-century chinoiserie panels from a château in Belgium before commissioning the Parisian decorator Henri Samuel to rethink the entire décor of the duplex. Inspired by the panels, Samuel decided to create a lavish indoor garden room, and called upon the renowned craftsmen of Atelier Mériguet-Carrère to have the panels incorporated into faux-latticework walls beneath a coffered dome. Samuel was, famously, a master of mixing contemporary and antique pieces. Here he placed a Giacometti coffee table on the antique Bessarabian rug and surrounded it with sumptuously reupholstered vintage wicker armchairs from a Danish palace. The pièce de résistance is the early nineteenth-century chinoiserie ironstone mantel.

Mrs. Gutfreund is a great hostess, and when she welcomes you into this enchanting room you leave New York far behind. While it is formal, it is also chic, comfortable, and filled with flowers. I have witnessed firsthand Mrs. Gutfreund enjoying the hunt for fine antiques and objets d'art at the stands of the finest dealers at fairs here and abroad, so I can truly appreciate how knowledgeable and passionate she is about the decorative arts.

Howard Slatkin

QUINTESSENTIAL NEW YORKER Howard S. Slatkin is a decorator of the old school, and his former six-thousand-square-foot aerie on upper Fifth Avenue in Manhattan is testimony to his awesome talent in re-creating eighteenth-century French interiors.

When Slatkin went into business years ago, his first employee was Carmen Almon, and they remain close friends. Almon married a French sculptor and moved to Bordeaux, where she makes astoundingly lifelike "portraits" of flowering plants, using copper sheeting, brass tubing, wire, and enamel paint. In the entrance hall of Slatkin's apartment, he understandably gave pride of place to Almon's flowering fruit tree branches.

The walls are papered in a vintage grisaille French scenic paper that was a gift from Slatkin's mother. The floors are covered in old limestone pavers. Ornamental plasterwork was applied to the ceiling. The antique carved French doors came from Jayne Wrightsman's estate in Palm Beach. Slatkin celebrates the craftsmen who work with him—these interiors, works of art unto themselves, took eleven years to produce. The designer has since moved downtown, but one can only hope that the current owner has left this magical space as it was designed.

EIGHTEENTH-CENTURY GRANDEUR
Howard Slatkin

THE CORNER OF decorator Howard Slatkin's
magnificent living room, which is forty feet by
thirty feet, with an eleven-foot-high ceiling, has
windows facing west to Central Park and south, so
it captures the feeling of being in the sunny salon
of a French château.

Unconventionally, Slatkin installed the parquet de
Versailles floor upside down and stained it white to
match the wall paneling, moldings, and Louis XVI
marble mantel. In this softly lit setting the gilt-wood
French eighteenth-century chairs, antique fire screen,
sconces, and candlesticks literally glow. The deep
purple sofa and thick lavender curtains add a regal
note to a room where every surface displays treasures
accumulated over a lifetime. It took Slatkin years to
gut, renovate, and decorate this remarkable apartment. Then, deciding he wanted to live in a town
house, he sold it in 2015. How could he? It was long
considered one of the very best designed apartments
in Manhattan.

Huniford Design Studio

NEW YORK DESIGNER James "Ford" Huniford accepted the challenge posed by a financier client who bought a penthouse in New York's Nolita (the area north of Little Italy). A wellness enthusiast, the client wanted a holistic sanctuary for his family and himself. In order to comply with his client's wishes, Huniford sought the advice of a certified building biology consultant and a fêng shui master.

For the kitchen, Huniford used reclaimed barn wood and repurposed metal cabinet doors, and he installed a raw-edge concrete countertop. The light fixtures are made with hexagons of natural mica. In some interiors designed with wellness in mind, the decorating is not of the same quality as the organic materials used, but that is certainly not the case here. This space is calm, modern, *and* organic.

DARK GLAMOUR

Ike Kligerman Barkley

SINCE 1989, the New York– and San Francisco–based architecture firm Ike Kligerman Barkley has been producing luxurious houses and interiors in a variety of styles, from classical to modern, in places from Sagaponack to Hawaii. Many clients are repeats, including a financier and his wife who bought two Fifth Avenue apartments in 2014 and asked partner Tom Kligerman to gut and combine them. Then they made an unusual request: "Unlike their other residences, they wanted black wood paneling in the entrance hall, dining room, family room, and kitchen," Kligerman recalls. "So, we chose to create a Moderne, urbane apartment, one that looked as if it had roots in the Manhattan of the 1930s, one you might see in a Fred Astaire movie." The result is undeniably elegant.

Materials in the glamorous black dining room are all new. The walls are paneled in sandblasted, wire-brushed pine that is heavily stained black. The doors and moldings are quarter-sawed walnut. "I wanted to give the room two scales, so I stopped the paneling ten inches below the ceiling and installed a fluted plaster frieze and recessed ceiling," Kligerman explains. The Beacon crystal pendants and sconces were designed and made by the New York artisan Alison Berger. The floor is oak, laid down in a chevron pattern with a scarified granite border. "It's all very black tie in feeling," notes Kligerman.

Ingrao Inc.

IN 1982, when New York designer Tony Ingrao opened his office in a town house on the Upper East Side, people swarmed to see it because it was unlike any other architect's or decorator's space. Arrayed in the pristine duplex with its white walls and white marble floors were exquisite antiques of all eras and origins: eighteenth-century English consoles, Venetian mirrors, French commodes, and Old Master paintings. A former antiques dealer, Ingrao has eclectic taste and refuses to be pegged to any particular style. He is as comfortable designing an eighteenth-century-style French château in Greenwich as he is a luminous contemporary interior, like the one he did for fashion designer Lisa Perry and her husband.

In 2002, when the couple bought all the penthouse apartments in one of the best addresses on Sutton Place—some sixty-four-hundred square feet—Ingrao suggested stripping out the neoclassical architecture and installing a minimalist shell with huge picture windows. Working with David Piscuskas of 1100 Architect, he created a futuristic space for the couple's large collection of Pop art. In the forty-foot-wide living room, Ingrao put in white lacquer walls, white marble floors, and custom white leather sofas to highlight a huge Roy Lichtenstein painting—and the view of the 59th Street Bridge outside. "I was inspired by the conversation pits of the 1960s," Ingrao says. "They come from the same period as the art."

Irvine & Fleming

KEITH IRVINE—the Scottish-born, New York–based decorator—died in 2011, but his English-style rooms in New York live on, still much loved by their owners. The foyer of this town house shows Irvine's mastery of Georgian style: warm, strong colors; overscaled printed textiles; deeply carved moldings; and eighteenth-century English antiques, including a magnificent carved eagle console.

The unusual black-and-white marble floor, set to a pattern of dancing rhythms, also proves that it's a design by Irvine: it's original, whimsical, and unique. Designer Mario Buatta, who worked as Irvine's assistant many decades ago, commented in 2008, "We all borrow from the Old World, but Keith has the knack of the real Englishman. His settings are a little more dramatic, a little more idiosyncratic. He has flair."

Jamie Drake

THE DINING ROOM in Gracie Mansion, the official residence of the mayor of New York, is in the oldest part of the house that Archibald Gracie built on the East River in 1799. It has also been the cause of some rueful decorating tales.

In 1984, during the Ed Koch administration, Albert Hadley was asked to oversee the mansion's redecoration, along with Mark Hampton. Assigned to the dining room, Hadley selected the 1830 scenic wallpaper by Zuber, Les Jardins Francais, but much of his plan was never realized. When the carpet installers arrived to install the green moiré patterned carpet Hadley ordered, the ladies of the Gracie Mansion Conservancy told them to replace it with a striped carpet that had been ordered for another room. Hadley resigned at once, saying the ladies "could play house" as they wished.

In 2002, Mayor Michael Bloomberg initiated a $7 million restoration of the mansion, employing his longtime decorator Jamie Drake of Drake Anderson to oversee the project. In the dining room Drake added the new pale striped green satin curtains and French Empire chandelier. A descendant of Archibald Gracie donated the antique rosewood Empire buffet, which has been attributed to Duncan Phyfe.

"The dining room is totally asymmetrical," notes Paul Gunther, executive director of the Conservancy today, "which just adds to its charm."

Jennifer Post Design

NEW YORK INTERIOR DESIGNER Jennifer Post has lived in the landmarked 1908 Apthorp on Broadway on the Upper West Side for decades. In fact, she is so fond of the Italian Renaissance Revival building that she kept moving within the building until she found her ideal space, an apartment with twelve-foot ceilings that stretches sixty feet from the building's central courtyard to its westernmost wall.

In 2016, she did a gut renovation of the space, covering the walls in luminous, soft white Venetian plaster and installing Bianco Dolomiti marble floors. She designed a sideboard to float above the floor next to the fireplace and commissioned a custom coffee table, rug, and the David Weeks chandelier. While Post certainly appreciates the building's original architecture and its history (residents have included George Balanchine, Nora Ephron, Conan O'Brien, and Cyndi Lauper), at home she prefers her signature twenty-first-century minimalism, especially since she is a serious collector of contemporary art, including the dancing bronze hares by Barry Flanagan.

Joanne De Palma Incorporated

VETERAN NEW YORK DESIGNER Joanne De Palma had the patience and commitment to take on a multiyear project for beloved clients who live in a landmarked late-nineteenth-century building on Central Park West. The couple wanted to furnish their duplex with late-nineteenth-century period pieces and was involved in the long hunt for appropriate antiques, including period lighting and works of art.

For the cavernous library, De Palma began with the rug. "I wanted a rug with clear colors that would lift the original dark millwork," she says. She found an antique Donegal carpet from circa 1900 in teal blue and vibrant green with a floral border, and knew it was perfect. "The colors are so vivid I knew I had to design a custom wall and curtain fabric, and logically thought of William Morris; I adapted a Morris pattern to go with the rug."

She glazed the cornice and ceiling in layers of pale blues and greens; hung an American circa-1860 large harp-form hall pendant lamp; added a fringed Carlo Bugatti chair with brass, copper, and pewter inlay; and located a pair of late-nineteenth-century ebonized library benches with lion-monopodium legs. The round center table with the painted columnar base is Italian, circa 1830. The charming French circa-1860 diorama behind the sofa has carved wood songbirds perched in a tree. The room is enchanting by day, and wildly romantic by night.

John Saladino

IN THE MID-1980S, New York designer John Saladino purchased the former ballroom of financier Jay Gould's five-story 1930s penthouse. Saladino renovated the whole floor, removing earlier alterations and restoring the original architectural details, in his effort to create a comfortable home for his family. Nearly three stories high, the square living room had enormous windows beneath the ceiling that faced north. Below them were French doors leading to Juliet balconies on 72nd Street.

Saladino loves Rome, having apprenticed there with architect Piero Sartogo, so he experimented with ways to make walls look like a modern Roman ruin. "The feeling of age and decay was achieved by mixing instant coffee with plaster, and then turning on the radiators full blast so that parts of the walls dried faster than others, resulting in a patina in which the color varied from dark taupe to pale bone," he explains. He hung pale gossamer shades over the huge north-south windows. Into this shell he added pastel-colored sofas, armchairs, and lamps of his own design, and oversized Italian antiques, including a seventeen-foot-long refectory table and a carved wooden Italian-style armchair that he guesses was a stage prop. The mixture of soft colors, muted light, and varied textures gave the room a magical atmosphere.

John Saladino

JOHN SALADINO, a veteran interior designer who works out of California and New York, is a master at creating illusion, perhaps something he learned during his time living in Rome.

For the dining room of what he calls his Manhattan client's "Venetian palace," Saladino commissioned French artist Jean Charles Dicharry to paint a Pompeiian-like garden mural with fruit trees, birds, and a lattice fence. After Dicharry had completed the painting, Saladino took a wet rag and distressed the base of the mural to create the effect of age and rising damp. The cool palette of beige and pale green and the antique French column fragments contribute to the outdoor feeling of the space. The mural exaggerates the dimensions of the room, while the beautifully laid table gives it human scale. You could almost be in Venice.

Juan Pablo Molyneux

IN 1983, the Chilean-born, Buenos Aires–based architect Juan Pablo Molyneux and his wife, Pilar, moved to New York. Using his classical training at the École nationale supérieure des Beaux-Arts in Paris, his unfettered imagination, and his insatiable curiosity, Molyneux has since designed everything from a romantic Russian palace in Quebec to a Palladian villa outside Moscow. He is a classicist who has sought out master craftsmen around the world to produce custom lacquer work, decorative painting, cabinetry, plasterwork, and embroidered textiles for the residences of his discerning clients.

In 2013, he finished a complete renovation of his own house: a seven-story 1885 brownstone on 69th Street between Park and Madison. He employed his favorite artisans to install the new black-and-white marble floor on the landing of the second floor, the piano nobile, and fabricate the bronze glass doors (made by the restorers of similar doors at Versailles) that lead into the living room. For the staircase walls, he commissioned Anne Midavaine of Atelier Midavaine in Paris to create scenic lacquered wood panels. "The naval battle scenes are based on a famous sixteenth-century Namban lacquered Japanese screen housed in the Museu Nacional de Arte Antiga in Lisbon," Molyneux says. "It depicts the arrival of the Portuguese fleet in Japan in 1543; they were the first Europeans to get there." Molyneux designed the console with square columns, he says, "to pay homage" to Claude Nicolas Ledoux, the visionary French eighteenth-century neoclassical architect. It all makes for a jaw-dropping entrance.

Juan Pablo Molyneux

WHEN A COSMOPOLITAN COUPLE purchased an East 66th Street apartment in 2012, they asked New York architect and designer Juan Pablo Molyneux to produce a spectacular living room—the wife, who is on the board of the New York City Ballet, and her husband, a distinguished banker, often entertain as many as two hundred for cocktails.

To create the spectacle, first Molyneux had to correct the symmetry of the room. The twenty-foot-high ceiling had only one beam and it was not centered, so he added others for balance and then installed a gold-and-white cornice. The red wall panels, inspired by a Coromandel screen he once saw in the embassy of the United States in Paris, are actually painted on canvas that was then glued to the walls. Molyneaux commissioned the Atelier Mériguet-Carrère, the design house that restored the Élysée Palace and the Palais Garnier in Paris, to create them. The panels were set into gold frames as if belonging to a Louis XV interior, but they, too, are trompe l'oeil, as is the gold chair rail.

The New York glass artist Miriam Ellner painted the gold verre églomisé lattice frame on the mirror over the mantel "as you would see in English chinoiserie," Molyneux says. When asked about inspiration for the mirror, he declares, "It was instantaneous. I needed to put something on those tall walls!" The gilt bronze rococo sconces are the real thing, as are the massive eighteenth-century terra-cotta globes with serpent bases, which were found in Italy. "One represents knowledge and the other the celestial sky," he explains. They are unusual but eye-stopping accents in a supremely glamorous room.

Juan Pablo Molyneux

JUAN PABLO MOLYNEUX is renowned for his opulent, palatial interiors, but he is equally comfortable creating modern apartments in contemporary buildings. When a client bought the fifty-fifth-floor penthouse in a residential tower on the East Side, Molyneux says he was challenged by the height of the fifteen-foot ceilings and the problem of containing the views of the East River and Queens. "Here you are, flying above New York as if you are in a plane," he says.

To make the dining room more intimate, he lined the walls and the soffit above the window in mahogany and installed a leather herringbone floor of the same color. The turquoise-colored ceramic oval dining table once belonged to the French comic actor Fernandel. Its rope-like legs are silhouetted against a white rug. The birch folding chairs are a contemporary version of a classical Italian Empire model, which Molyneaux upholstered in chocolate silk velvet. The round bronze sculpture by Bruno Romeda frames the glittering nighttime view to the east.

Julian Schnabel

PERHAPS ONLY AN ARTIST would have the audacity to build a fifty-thousand-square-foot Italian palazzo on top of a former stable in Greenwich Village, but that is what the Brooklyn-born painter and filmmaker Julian Schnabel did at 360 West 11th Street.

In the 1980s he rented a studio in the former six-story stable. Then he bought it in 1997. By 2008 he had built nine full floors on top of the roof, paying attention to every detail from curtain rods, door handles, and finials to the swimming pool. No detail was too large or too small. An admirer of Giotto's frescoes in the Scrovegni Chapel in Padua and the Mediterranean Revival houses of Addison Mizner in Palm Beach, Schnabel added a stuccoed pink façade with archways and terraces. Interior walls were lined with rough-hewn, recycled wood or layered with hand-applied plaster. The floors boast colorful vintage ceramic tiles. The seven hundred balusters made for the bronze handrails involved casting molten metal in sand molds and then grinding, sanding, milling, and applying patina. Schnabel still lives and works in the palazzo. His pink bedroom, here dominated by Picasso's *Femme au Chapeau* (1971), is decorated with Italian antiques and a glittering chandelier. It's Venice in New York.

THE FLOW OF COLOR

Katie Ridder

NEW YORK DESIGNER Katie Ridder and her husband, the acclaimed classical architect Peter Pennoyer, do not often have the chance to work together, but when they do, they enjoy the collaboration.

This living room was created when Pennoyer gutted and combined three apartments on Fifth Avenue for an investment banker and his wife. When it came to decorating, Ridder was especially cognizant of her clients' fine art collection. For the living room, she created lavender walls with a shimmering paint that incorporates pearlescent mica dust "so it wouldn't look dead," Ridder explains. The luminous lavender seems to extend the sky of the Kiki Smith painting, and serves as a calm background for the many layers of pattern throughout the room: the ash and beige linen-weave sofa, the Indian mother-of-pearl-inlaid coffee tables, the antique Tabriz carpet, and the embroidered orange velvet upholstery on the Swedish armchair. Ridder says the orange accent started with the trim on the lavender silk curtains (not seen here), and continued with the silk pillows and the piping on the club chairs.

Ridder is known for her unusual palettes of primary and secondary colors, as exemplified by the unique lavender-orange combination seen here. As she notes: "I'm very interested in color flow as you move through a space."

Katie Ridder

WHEN KATIE RIDDER was asked to reconfigure an apartment in a former Gimbels department store on East 86th Street, she was faced with a challenge: the dining room was an awkward, small space with no windows that was stuck between the entrance hall and the living room.

But, she had an ingenious solution—to bring in daylight, she commissioned new doors with custom Bendheim glass panes in pale beige, lavender, green, and blue. That set the palette for her beige printed grass-cloth wallpaper, the robin's-egg-blue leather chairs that she designed, the zebrawood vintage dining table, the vintage crystal waterfall chandelier, and the English Arts and Crafts carpet.

Andreas Gursky's large-scale photograph of the Grand Hyatt Shanghai hotel lobby came later, the perfect finishing touch, the yellow complementing the blue chairs. This dining room is an example of Ridder's mastery of color; it is alluring even when it's empty. Similarly bright colors in unusual combinations are also seen in Ridder's own line of fabric and wallpapers. The cheerful prints have names like Moonflower, Pagoda, Peony, and Beetlecat (an old-fashioned sailboat). The patterns on the rugs she designs are equally striking and colorful.

KLC Studios and Peter Pennoyer Architects

IN 2010, one of New York's most prominent collectors of Americana bought a triplex on Fifth Avenue. Because the building is narrow, his wife decided the top floor, which has terraces overlooking Central Park and the Upper East Side, would be her husband's private lair—a combined library and bedroom. She went to her friend Katie Leede of KLC Studios and architect Peter Pennoyer to rebuild the space from scratch.

"I wanted to make it timeless, so it didn't look decorated," Leede says. After Pennoyer hid all the mechanicals in the ceiling, she paneled it. She then started with the Gilbert Stuart portrait of George Washington ("one of the best and rarest"). Under it is an early-eighteenth-century French serpentine marble mantel she found in London. She lined the walls with beige suede panels and installed a lush wool rug to give the space "Old World quiet." She designed the bed with hand-spun linen. Because the collector's wife loves antique textiles, for the club chairs Leede commissioned a couturier's embroiderer to copy the foliage on an eighteenth-century Portuguese crewel-work towel. The stool is nineteenth-century Italian with Moorish mashrabiya-style sides.

The result is a luxe space for reading and contemplation. "It feels like a Parisian pied-à-terre," Leede comments.

Lela Rose and Work Architecture Company (WORKac)

TEXAS-BORN LELA ROSE is not your average New York fashion designer, and beyond the stylish dresses she is known for, she also embraces avant-garde architecture. When Rose and her husband bought a six-thousand-square-foot maisonette in a former 1865 department store in Tribeca, they commissioned two former graduates of Rem Koolhaas's OMA (the Office of Metropolitan Architecture), who had formed their own company in 2003, Work Architecture Company (WORKac). Rose's brief: design an apartment for a young family of four.

It took four years for Dan Wood of WORKac to devise the upside-down triplex with public rooms on the street level atop two basement floors. The minimalist, dramatic living room with sixteen-foot ceilings and a white resin floor is furnished with vintage gray Pierre Paulin sectionals, a gray rug, and a white John Dickinson side table with paw feet. Rose's personal photographs are installed salon-style on the back wall.

This space was designed to be multifunctional, perfect for throwing huge parties and for Rose to present her dress collections: a section of the glass ceiling descends at the push of a button to become a dining table. It can also be joined to a long Japanese-style wooden table set in the floor of the bamboo-clad room next door that rises via a scissor lift. Together the tables become a catwalk for Rose's fashion models—or a table that can seat sixty-eight for dinner.

CLASSIC SIMPLICITY

MAC II and Bill Blass

THE FOYER OF THE LATE fashion legend Bill Blass's Sutton Place apartment is the essence of classicism—an octagonal room with a graphic flooring of white pavers bound by wooden frames that organizes a balanced arrangement of antiques: pairs of chairs, book cabinets, bronze horse sculptures, and architectural drawings.

Blass worked on the apartment with friends and noted interior designers Chessy Rayner and Mica Ertegun of the firm MAC II. Ertegun notes, "Bill owned the most amazing antique furniture, art, and statuary that he had collected in his travels around the world. He wanted to have large open areas to best show his collection. I thought the space needed an interesting gallery entry, which became the shape of an octagon. Since there was a structural column in the space that could not be removed, we resolved the issue by creating a second column on the opposite side and clad them both with plaster to resemble a pair of Doric columns. The result pleased Bill, who worked closely with Chessy and me on the entire project." It was a collaboration made in heaven.

SQUARE PERFECTION

MAC II and Bill Blass

THE MAIN LIVING SPACE in Bill Blass's Sutton Place apartment was spare, devoid of color, filled with natural daylight—and impossibly chic.

A large Picasso drawing hung above the fireplace, taking pride of place in a space filled with busts, ancient Greek and Roman torsos, mounted cameos, and a pair of Regency daybeds with striped upholstery. (A native of Indiana, Blass was always called the all-American designer, but here the feeling was more British.) The combined living room and dining room was thirty feet square. "I moved in solely because of the height of the ceilings and the size of the rooms, and because they were square," Blass wrote. "I mean, square is the perfect shape for a room." The fashion designer worked with MAC II, the firm of Mica Ertegun and Chessy Rayner, in the design of his perfect rooms.

A BEDROOM TO DREAM IN

MAC II and Bill Blass

BILL BLASS, who died in 2002 at seventy-nine, once said, "I have always thought fashion designers are the best interior decorators. I love it. It's all a question of the eye; you are soliciting the same innate talent."

His Sutton Place apartment was spare, with a mostly muted palette. His taste was impeccable, but he also got help at home from decorators Chessy Rayner and Mica Ertegun, of MAC II. The bedroom, its bed upholstered in red paisley, also served as a library, museum, and gallery for his collection of drawings and Grand Tour souvenirs. The enormous antique mahogany center table boasted a bronze replica of Trajan's column in Rome, antique globes, books, and beautifully crafted antique architectural models. Not far from a much-used leather wing chair was a large bronze of a soldier astride a horse, sword at his side. "What I have here is the result of a lifetime of collecting," Blass wrote. "There is no relationship between the things themselves—except I like them." He continued, "When I collect things, I choose how they are going to look in my life. The way I decorated here was to surround myself with the things I love . . . and they all have great dignity."

A TORTOISESHELL SANCTUARY
Marilyn Evins

MARILYN EVINS, the late Manhattan public-relations dynamo, was renowned for her great taste and sense of style. This is clearly evident in her apartment in The Pierre.

Evins had a vision for it. When she bought the apartment, it had been unoccupied for thirty years, so she gutted it, changed the layout, and decorated it with her French antiques and Impressionist paintings. She then asked the talented muralist Erik Filban to cover the walls in glowing butterscotch faux tortoiseshell inspired by her most prized antique, a French vernis Martin faux-tortoiseshell commode. It took him months to finish, alternating layers of colored varnishes, but he achieved a fiery palette. A Louis XV mirror reigns above a French eighteenth-century lit de repos. The Régence dining room chairs were used for the small dinners Evins liked to host in the library, when she would cover the table with a rich brocade and set it with Chinese export famille rose porcelain plates and Baccarat crystal. Only the bookcases, designed by Billy Baldwin, are modern, testaments to her belief in mixing styles and periods.

Mario Buatta

MARIO BUATTA, the popular society decorator affectionately called "the Prince of Chintz," is a master at creating wonderfully cheerful English country house interiors for sophisticated city dwellers. He is equally beloved for his wit. "What does it take to be a good decorator?" he asks. "You have to be an actor (to pretend you like the client), a psychiatrist (to figure out what he wants), and a lawyer (to collect your fees)."

Buatta infuses his rooms with color and warmth, texture and comfort. This midtown penthouse, which once belonged to the celebrity chronicler Earl Blackwell, is seven thousand square feet and boasts a fifty-foot-long living room.

For its tycoon owner, Buatta injected new, classic interior architecture to the living room, adding a hefty cornice to frame the silver-leafed, barrel-vault ceiling, as well as overscaled, faux marble pediments over the doors, and a new, mirrored fireplace surround. The apple-green walls create a festive atmosphere, while the grand silk draperies add drama and glamour. The room is designed for entertaining on a large scale, which explains the wide array of antiques, contemporary case furniture, and comfortable upholstered pieces. "Color is important," Buatta says—he is one of the few decorators today who has not abandoned strong tones, vibrant prints, and layered ornamentation. And why should he?

MASTERFUL UNDERSTATEMENT
Mark Hampton

BEFORE HIS UNTIMELY DEATH in 1998, the beloved New York decorator Mark Hampton had a rollicking and diverse three-decade career, catering to elite clients, painting watercolors (one became the 1983 White House Christmas card), and writing about design. He was renowned for his public work at the White House, Blair House, and the American Academy in Rome, as well as the interiors he designed for prestigious clients, including Lord Palumbo, Henry Kravis, and Estée Lauder. Nonetheless, one of his favorite projects was the eleven-room apartment he designed in 1990 for his friends Susan and Carter Burden at 1020 Fifth Avenue, one of the most desirable prewar buildings in Manhattan—the building was designed by Warren & Wetmore, the architects of Grand Central Terminal.

The forty-by-twenty-one-foot combined drawing room and library with eighteen-foot-tall ceilings is particularly spectacular. Here, the dapper Hampton worked on the architecture with Oscar Shamamian of Ferguson & Shamamian and master craftsman Gregory Gurfein, who fabricated the mahogany bookcases for the Burdens' rare book collection. While it is opulent, this room is all about comfort, with red wool walls, French and English antiques, and a huge Oriental rug.

"The one threat is that of looking pretentious," Hampton once wrote. "Understatement is a pain in the neck sometimes, but it is a good thing to keep in mind, even when you are contemplating some ravishing excess."

Mark Hampton

THIS REMARKABLY PRETTY dining room in the penthouse of a venerable 1915 building on Park Avenue was one of thirteen rooms that Mark Hampton decorated for a society grande dame. Hampton was asked to re-create the atmosphere of the sprawling horse country estate in New Jersey where she had grown up, which had been filled with chintz, antiques, and fine pictures. He papered the walls of the dining room in a trellis design that had originally come from France, as did the nineteenth-century silver and crystal chandelier. Atop the fireplace surround, he placed a magnificent blanc de Chine chinoiserie overmantel mirror sporting human figures, squirrels, sea shells, and pagoda roofs. A pair of eighteenth-century English gilt-wood wall lights flanks the mirror. The seats of the Chippendale-style mahogany chairs are covered in a hand-blocked floral chintz depicting roses, lilacs, and dahlias. The owner's antique Georgian silverware and Chinese export porcelain, part of an eclectic collection of English antiques and Old Master paintings that the client inherited, are displayed on a crisp linen and silk damask tablecloth. It may be traditional, but it's a ravishing décor by an American master.

Mark Hampton

AFTER FINANCIER SAUL STEINBERG bought a thirty-four-room triplex penthouse at 740 Park Avenue—a favorite address of the Who's Who of New York—he commissioned Mark Hampton to reconfigure the hallways and add Georgian-inspired moldings and paneling to the public rooms.

The library, which also served as Steinberg's study, sends a powerful message with a huge treen statue of Atlas bearing the weight of the world, a white marble lion with its paw on a globe, bronze busts of famous figures from history, and neoclassical bas-relief roundels. The faux-bois cornices, wainscoting, and pilasters reflect the tones of the massive desk with appliquéd book spines. The ceiling is papered, enhancing the clubby, masculine feel of the room.

The apartment has quite a lineage. In the 1930s, '40s, and '50s, it belonged to John D. Rockefeller Jr. In 2000, Steinberg sold it (reportedly for $35 million, setting a record as the most expensive co-op ever at the time) to Blackstone CEO Stephen Schwarzman, who still calls it home.

Massimo and Lella Vignelli

NO ONE WHO HAS EVER visited the Upper East Side duplex of renowned Italian designers Massimo and Lella Vignelli, located in a 1907 Renaissance-style building, has forgotten it. The couple, admired and beloved for their partnership, Vignelli Associates, was also warm and funny and supportive of rising talent.

Although Mr. Vignelli was primarily a graphic artist most famous for the colorful 1972 New York City subway map and the signature Brown Bag shopping bags from Bloomingdale's, he and his wife were both rigorous modernists. This applied whether they were designing chairs, like the stackable Handkerchief chair for Knoll, glass-topped tables with massive bases for Acerbis, or melamine tableware.

In the double-height living room of their thirty-nine-hundred-square-foot duplex, which is bathed in light from a twenty-foot-high leaded-glass window, they lived with simple modern pieces, many of their own design: Mr. Vignelli designed the solid steel square table near the fireplace. Both designed the round center table. Much of the glassware they used every day was commissioned by Venini. Similarly, some of the furniture was from their time with Casigliani. It is said that the Vignellis designed something new every single day of their lives.

McKim, Mead & White

THE FRENCH EMBASSY'S Cultural Services building, on Fifth Avenue at 78th Street, contains one of the most glittering Gilded Age rooms in Manhattan: a mirrored reception hall with gold embellishments, a golden trellised cornice boasting porcelain flowers, swags of carved wood roses, and picture frames crowned with cupids. The elegant room, like the mansion, was designed by Stanford White of McKim, Mead & White. The residence was a wedding gift to the financier and sportsman Payne Whitney and his bride, Helen Hay, from Payne Whitney's uncle.

Not only is the five-story, Renaissance-style granite mansion considered one of Stanford White's finest buildings, but it is also one of his greatest interiors—he provided both the eighteenth-century European furnishings and the works of art. The room is now a landmark designated by the New York Landmarks Preservation Foundation.

Sadly, White was murdered before the house was finished in 1909 (final cost was thought to be $1 million). The mirrored reception room was Helen Hay Whitney's favorite; she called it the "Venetian Room." Before she died in 1944, she made sure that the room would be preserved after her death. Her wishes were followed in 1948, when the room was dismantled and put in storage. Her son John Hay ("Jock") Whitney sold the house in 1949. The French government bought it in 1952 to use as a cultural outpost of the French Embassy in New York. In 1997 Betsey Cushing Roosevelt Whitney, Jock's widow, donated the Venetian Room to the French-American Foundation and provided the funds to have it reinstalled in its original home at 972 Fifth Avenue. Because the mansion also houses the Albertine, a charming French bookshop, the lobby is open to the public during business hours, so visitors can catch a glimpse of the reception room next door.

Michael S. Smith Inc. and Ferguson & Shamamian Architects

MUCH LIKE AN eighteenth-century French château, the living room of this Central Park South aerie has windows on two facing sides, with northern and southern exposures, so it is always flooded with natural light. That is what prompted longtime clients of designer Michael S. Smith to buy the apartment, which was, at the time, a gutted shell.

"The view was omnipresent, and we wanted to maximize the light, to keep it bright and cheerful in a city that can be very gray," Smith says. So, he and his frequent collaborator Oscar Shamamian created new architecture with Venetian plaster walls, lacquered coffers in the eleven-foot-tall ceiling, and classical moldings. "White can be a bit one-note," Smith explains, "so we wanted to add more dimension." This involved mixing pearl gray, cream, white, and lavender to the paint to make the room glow, an effect enhanced by the parquet floor, which was hand-hammered with German silver. Shamamian commissioned the floor from artisans in India. A Franz Kline painting hangs on top of a watery mirror handmade in the Czech Republic. The gilt wood Treviso armchairs are from Smith's furniture line, Jasper. The parchment-lined stools were bought at auction.

Michael S. Smith Inc. and Ferguson & Shamamian Architects

FOR THE DINING ROOM of this Central Park South apartment, Michael S. Smith commissioned Féau & Cie of Paris to make custom cast and carved plaster wall panels. The panels are replicates of an eighteenth-century model that had been repurposed in the 1960s by the eminent French decorating firm Maison Jansen. (Jansen helped First Lady Jacqueline Kennedy in the White House until it was deemed unpatriotic for her to hire foreign designers.)

The chalk-white, limewashed plaster is a perfect background for the Brice Marden painting; Louis XVI–style chairs from Smith's furniture line, Jasper; the antique French mahogany dining table; and a pair of commodes made in 1778 for the Château de Bagatelle in the Bois de Boulogne, Paris. What keeps the room modern and unstuffy are the boxy, crystal contemporary lamps by Christophe Côme and Andy Warhol's silkscreen *Knives*.

Michael S. Smith Inc. and Ferguson & Shamamian Architects

MICHAEL S. SMITH, the California-based decorator best known for his work in the Obama White House, has an extremely loyal clientele that includes Rupert Murdoch, George Clooney, and Steven Spielberg. Smith had already designed five houses for one jet-setting couple when they acquired a sixth: an apartment in the Ritz-Carlton on Central Park South.

For the library, inspired by the legendary apartment of Coco Chanel, Smith bought an eighteenth-century Coromandel lacquer screen from Steinitz in Paris. Working with his friend, the architect Oscar Shamamian, Smith lined the room in French white oak and framed each antique panel. When the designers needed extra panels to fill out the space, they commissioned Féau & Cie in Paris to reproduce them, thereby creating a jewel box of a room. And a quiet one, too: the floor is covered in leather. This refined setting is perfect for a Russian neoclassical desk, an eighteenth-century commode, and two silk-upholstered bergères. This library is both cozy and highly refined.

Miles Redd

NEW YORK DECORATOR Miles Redd probably has the only bathroom in Manhattan that can—and regularly does—seat ten for dinner. It is a historic bathroom as well, one that the renowned Chicago architect David Adler designed in 1931 with his sister, interior designer Frances Elkins.

In 1998, Redd spotted two antique mirrored doors in a Chicago salvage warehouse and learned that they were from the famous Lake Bluff, Illinois, mansion where meatpacking heir Lester Armour lived with his glamorous second wife, Princess Alexandra "Aleka" Pavlovna Galitzine Romanoff Armour. The doors belonged to a bathroom with four walls and a ceiling covered in Directoire-style mirrored paneling, which was disassembled when pop singer Richard Marx bought the mansion and gutted it. Thankfully, the warehouse preserved it in its entirety.

"It seemed like a distant pipe dream," Redd recalls, "to have a famous bathroom by a famous architect. I decided to buy it, and put it on hold for a week. And when I was late in calling back and learned that it had been sold to someone else, I begged to be contacted if the sale fell through.'"

Two months later, Redd got his bathroom, and the timing was perfect; he was busy renovating a Federal town house for himself and his sister Sarah's family. "All the plans for the bathroom were on microfiche in the Adler archive, carefully detailed by the person who had taken it down." This information was essential for the re-installation, which was an arduous process, especially as some of the panels had to be repaired. But it was one that provided him years of pleasure and satisfaction. "A mirrored bath doesn't come along twice in a lifetime," he notes. It is impossibly glam.

Mott B. Schmidt

THE PHILANTHROPIST and banker David Rockefeller
may have been a billionaire, but he, his wife, Peggy, and
their six children lived quietly for many decades in the
double-width redbrick Colonial Revival town house at
146 East 65th Street. They bought the house in 1948 and
hired Mott B. Schmidt, a popular classical architect with
whom they had already worked, to make alterations.
Schmidt most likely introduced the pine paneling to the
forty-foot-wide living room with oversize windows on the
second floor.

Here, the Rockefellers created a homey atmosphere for
entertaining and enjoying their first-rate Impressionist
and modern paintings, antique Chinese and European
porcelains, pre-Columbian ceramics, and English
antiques. The room, famously, was home to Cézanne's
Boy in a Red Vest (since given to the Museum of Modern
Art) and Seurat's *La Rade de Grandcamp*. Exceptional
antiques included a pair of George II library armchairs
with tapestry upholstery, a magnificent Irish George II
mahogany armchair, a Queen Anne walnut bureau
cabinet, and a pair of Queen Anne walnut stools.

AN EXOTIC ENTRANCE

Neil Adam Mackay

IN 2005, five years before he died at age ninety-five, John W. Kluge, the immigrant from Germany who became a billionaire communications entrepreneur, moved into a new Fifth Avenue apartment with his fourth wife, Maria Tussi Kuttner Kluge.

The apartment was not large, but British designer Neil Adam Mackay made it look very grand. Of his multiple skills, Mackay enjoys painting most. The Kluges had worked with him before and appreciated his ability to paint murals, trompe l'oeil backgrounds, and faux-painted tapestries.

A large glazed Qing-dynasty temple guardian—Kluge collected modern paintings and almost anything that was antique (Indian, Chinese, Greek, Etruscan, Aboriginal, and Egyptian works of art)—is the only "real" thing in the colorful entrance hall. The pilasters have been faux marbled, and the elaborate parquetry design on the floor has been painted to look like an intricate mosaic of several varieties of rare wood. The pattern "is based on one in a St. Petersburg palace," Mackay explains. The colors of the faux marble and the floor are picked out in the moldings, and the faux-trellis decorative painting graces both walls and ceiling, making the entry quite fancy but also intimate.

Parish-Hadley

OF THE FOURTEEN ROOMS in Brooke Astor's duplex with six terraces at 778 Park Avenue, the library was her favorite—perhaps because it symbolized her passionate and generous support of the New York Public Library. And yet Parish-Hadley's stunning design almost never happened.

After Vincent Astor died in 1959, Mrs. Astor moved into the duplex. She had Parish-Hadley decorate the entire space, but one room was little altered: the library retained its Louis XV–style boiserie. Here, Parish-Hadley supplied comfortable sofas and armchairs and added a fine antique Bessarabian carpet to anchor the room. In the late 1970s, Mrs. Astor reportedly invited Albert Hadley to tea to deliver some bad news: she had decided to ask the preeminent English decorator Geoffrey Bennison to reimagine the library. Thinking quickly, Hadley told her to replace the wood paneling with something sleek and modern—red lacquered walls with brass-trimmed floor-to-ceiling bookshelves, which would be perfect to display her late husband's fine collection of rare books. She loved the idea, and never hired Bennison. Hadley had the walls lacquered (supposedly ten times) and added an antique brass clock, ancient sculptures such as the Tang camel, and fine American paintings. It was a comfortable, cozy, and chic setting for the doyenne of New York society to entertain First Ladies and friends from every stratum of society.

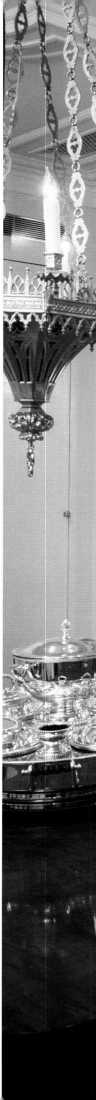

Parish-Hadley and Ferguson & Shamamian Architects

IN THE 1990S, when a couple, collectors of contemporary art, bought an apartment on Fifth Avenue, they picked their dream team to work on it: Oscar Shamamian and Albert Hadley, who worked with Brian Murphy on the decoration.

A classicist, Shamamian naturally appreciated the well-proportioned rooms of the 1920s Rosario Candela building, but he also knew the couple liked to entertain sixty for dinner, so he suggested creating a double dining room. By eliminating a staff room, he created a breakfast space that faces east, and enough room for extra dining tables. He stenciled a new floor to tie the spaces together, created an octagonal ceiling molding, and added pale green marble Corinthian columns to, as he puts it, "dematerialize" the room visually. "So many of our clients are art collectors that we end up putting a lot of architecture into ceilings, floors, and columns," he says.

He then worked with Hadley, mixing modern art with classical architecture and the couple's collection of English antiques, which includes a Robert Adam gilt-wood mirror. The painted trompe l'oeil curtains on the far wall are actually made of wood. They came from the venerable New York antiques shop Frederick P. Victoria & Son, Inc. Hadley had them fitted for the room—a whimsical addition to the classical space.

Patrick Naggar and Terese Carpenter (Nile, Inc.)

ONLY A SERIOUS COLLECTOR of ancient art, paintings by Old Masters, and fine antiques would go to a classically trained architect, who had graduated from the École nationale supérieure des Beaux-Arts in Paris, to design her East Side apartment. Patrick E. Naggar is a French architect, artist, and furniture designer (for Ralph Pucci International) whose work here reflects the synergy between sculpture and architecture.

Working in the late 1980s with his New York colleague, designer Terese Carpenter (the firm was then called Nile, Inc.), Naggar made the foyer the central room in the apartment, a temple-like gallery with beige walls to suggest limestone; a pitched, coffered ceiling to accommodate the huge bronze statue of Roman Emperor Lucius Verus (who reigned from A.D. 161 to 169 with his adoptive brother and co-ruler, Marcus Aurelius); and a black-and-white checkerboard marble floor on which to perch rows of black pedestals displaying Greek heads and Roman portrait busts. The effect is breathtaking.

A MODERN ICON ON BEEKMAN

Paul Rudolph

IN 1976, the modernist architect Paul Rudolph was able to purchase an entire five-story 1860s brick town house at 23 Beekman Place for $300,000, after renting an apartment there for several years. Over the next few years, he added a steel skeleton sheathed with glass and concrete-block panels to create a four-story fantasy penthouse on the top. By the time he got his Certificate of Occupancy in 1992, he had inserted twenty-seven levels into his dazzling penthouse, with various sitting areas, a kitchen, bathrooms, and a library whose ceiling soared three stories.

The materials he used were simple: The steel skeleton was clad in shiny white Formica. The floors were covered in reflective metal, Lucite, carpet, and glass. Moving from level to level was like a sobriety test; you could not look down or you might fall off the rail-free vertiginous staircase. But individual rooms grounded you with works of art, sculptures, and other treasured finds, all beautifully displayed, not unlike the way nineteenth-century architect Sir John Soane showcased his own collections in his neoclassical house in London.

Rudolph died in 1997. In 2000, young modernist collectors Michael and Gabrielle Boyd bought the house for $5.5 million and did a comprehensive restoration. When they moved to California in 2003, they sold it and the property has changed hands several times since. In 2010, when the house became a New York City historic landmark, Landmarks Preservation Commission chairman Robert Tierney called it a modern icon.

Pei Cobb Freed & Partners and Peter Marino Architect and Ty Warner

WHILE NEW YORK ARCHITECT Peter Marino is especially known for his work with the top fashion houses and luxury brands, creating boutiques for Chanel, Louis Vuitton, and Dior, he also works in the hospitality sector.

In 2004, the renowned architect I.M. Pei, for whom Marino had apprenticed, came out of retirement to work with Marino on the re-design of the entire fifty-second floor of the Four Seasons Hotel in New York (Pei had originally designed the hotel). Named the Ty Warner Penthouse after the hotel's owner, the forty-three-hundred-square-foot one-bedroom suite has a living room, library, Zen room, spa, breakfast room, and powder room. It also has four cantilevered glass balconies and unobstructed 360-degree views over Manhattan and Central Park.

For the seven-hundred-square-foot library, which has a twenty-six-foot-tall ceiling and diamond-shaped skylight, Pei and Marino had French artisans lacquer the walls a glossy caramel and then installed four floor-to-ceiling bookcases embellished with elaborate bronze leaves and tendrils fashioned by the Paris sculptor Claude Lalanne. They are complemented by the gilded bronze crocodile coffee table and branch chandelier, also by Lalanne. "I like art that's used," says Marino, who is crazy about bronze; he collects Renaissance and Baroque bronzes and designs bronze consoles that are sold in limited editions. The creation of the penthouse was a seven-year collaboration, and every detail was hand selected by Warner, Marino, and Pei.

Peter Pennoyer
Architects

MANHATTANITE TONY BLUMKA is the fourth
generation of his family to run the Blumka Gallery,
which specializes in medieval and Renaissance
works of art and sculpture. His great-grandfather
founded the firm in Vienna in the nineteenth
century. In 1939, Tony's father, Leopold, moved the
gallery to 57th Street in Manhattan. There he met
his future wife, Ruth, newly arrived from Munich,
when she wandered into the gallery one day, home-
sick to speak German.

Tony Blumka inherited the gallery in 1997 and
moved it to his own town house on East 72nd Street.
Peter Pennoyer designed and built the light-filled
sculpture gallery in the rear of the house, where
medieval bronzes, enamels, and statues are put
on view in constant rotation. Blumka Gallery is
private; it sells art by participating in shows like The
European Fine Art Fair (TEFAF). Blumka clients
include the Museum of Fine Arts, Boston, the Frick,
the Cleveland Museum of Art, and the J. Paul Getty.
It has also donated several pieces to the Metropolitan Museum of Art (Ruth Blumka and former
Met director Thomas Hoving were friends). Tony
Blumka is one of very few American dealers to have
been knighted by the French government with the
Ordre des Arts et des Lettres.

Philip Johnson

ONE OF THE FINEST houses the late architect Philip Johnson ever designed is probably his least known: a modern two-story town house with a simple brick and glass façade in the Turtle Bay section of Manhattan. A designated landmark, it was completed in 1950, just a year after his now-iconic Glass House in New Canaan, Connecticut. Blanchette Ferry Hooker Rockefeller, the wife of John D. Rockefeller III, commissioned it as a place to entertain and display works of art that her husband didn't much like (such as Alberto Giacometti's bronze *Man Pointing*). The house was halfway between the Rockefeller apartment on Beekman Place and the Museum of Modern Art (MoMA), where she twice served as president of the board, so it made for a convenient stop on her commute. The ground floor has a simple plan: the room in the front, with white brick walls and a white tile floor, connects via a pond with travertine pavers to a back room that, during the Rockefeller years, had a few club chairs and works of art. In the mid-1950s, Mrs. Rockefeller donated the house to MoMA. The house has been in several private hands since then.

Phillip Thomas Inc.

INTERIOR DESIGNER Phillip Thomas may have been born and reared in New York City, but his outlook is decidedly international. In fact, he chose to study design only after earning a degree in international relations. This no doubt came in handy in 2014 when a foreign couple bought what they call their "tree house on the Hudson"—a luxurious penthouse duplex with panoramic views in one of the Richard Meier–designed glass towers in Greenwich Village.

Everything is carefully orchestrated. "Since the apartment is exposed to an ever-changing landscape," Thomas says, "I designed it with a neutral palette to complement both mother nature and the carefully curated collection of art and furniture within. It had to be warm, cozy, and inviting, so there's lots of wood, metal, and leather." He is like a couturier—he commissioned Chris Lehrecke to craft the wooden shelves on the custom pearlescent leather-sheathed column. He installed wide-plank teak floors. He had Lesage of Paris embroider the dining room chairs, each in a different pattern. The gold drinks table is by French sculptor Philippe Hiquily. The beige sofas and chairs were chosen to complement the rug, which Thomas had woven in wool and silk swirls of putty, cream, and gray to simulate the currents in the Hudson River.

Renzo Mongiardino

THE LATE MILANESE interior architect Renzo Mongiardino was the master of creating magical transformations, something his illustrious clients—including the Agnelli and Rothschild families, Michel David-Weill, and Baron Thyssen-Bornemisza—all appreciated. He could take a raw space and create a whole environment, one that looked palatial, vaguely historical, comfortable, and just plain dazzling. His particularly inimitable skill was his ability to combine the real with the faux, using trompe l'oeil wood, stone, or marble finishes.

After Randolph Hearst married Veronica DeGruyter Beracasa de Uribe in 1982, as a wedding present he bought her a grand floor-through apartment in a twelve-story, limestone-clad 1920 co-op at Fifth Avenue and East 66th Street. They lived there until Randolph died (Veronica sold the apartment in 2002). Decorating the residence was one of the few projects that Renzo Mongiardino took on in Manhattan.

For the thirty-five-foot-long, twelve-foot-high entrance gallery, Mongiardino treated the walls with faux-marble panels of different colors. He was the master at creating artificial effects. The grand doors to the elevator landing are painted with Renaissance-style ornamental arabesque motifs not unlike those in the sixteenth-century Loggia of Raphael in the Apostolic Palace in the Vatican. Flanking the doors are ancient marble busts on pedestal columns. This is where the Hearsts famously welcomed Lady Diana and entertained other luminaries. It is a fine example of how Mongiardino guided his gifted artisans to give grandeur to a space through immeasurable creativity, an artistic application of paint, and superbly chosen artifacts.

Renzo Mongiardino

"ONE OF MY GROUND RULES is that there are no rules," the set decorator and Milanese interior architect Renzo Mongiardino once said. "When it comes down to it, you invent as you go along. You see a room, and you let it play around in your mind until the right solution starts to emerge."

For the living room of Veronica Hearst's floor-through apartment at 66th Street and Fifth Avenue, Mongiardino created a wall of hand-painted leather "tiles" whose colors were inspired by Italian Renaissance maiolica. (He could have had real tiles made, but where would the fun be in *that*?) They make an intriguing background for the Old Master painting hung above the mantelpiece, the jewel-toned tufted damask upholstery fabrics, and fine Oriental rug. On the other side of the salon, he inserted large lacquered chinoiserie panels between faux-bamboo columns in a room filled with velvet, deep-seated sofas, club chairs, and lavishly appointed coffee tables. Mongiardino was not only a master of illusion but also a master at creating the kind of warm ambiance that promotes intimate conversation.

Richard Keith Langham Inc.

WHEN ALABAMA-BORN, New York–based designer Richard Keith Langham was asked by his newly single friend to look at her recently purchased duplex in Gainsborough Studios on Central Park South, he told her it was one of the five best apartments in the city—to say nothing of its spectacular views of Central Park.

Though the client is a philanthropist with an active social schedule, she wanted her new apartment to be serene and somewhat informal. Uncharacteristically, Langham chose a pale, monochromatic pewter-gray and white palette to complement her superb collection of art and antiques, including a Régence commode, Russian fruitwood bergères, and a bust of Hercules that had once belonged to Bill Blass. Rock-crystal sconces and Lucite drinks tables add to the glamour, as does the tall mirror over the fireplace, which enlarges the already soaring space: a perfect thirty-foot square.

Trained by such legendary decorators as Mark Hampton and Keith Irvine, Langham has worked with many prominent ladies in the past, including Jacqueline Kennedy Onassis and Mrs. William F. Buckley Jr. This beautiful bachelorette apartment is in the same mold as some of his previous projects, but is uniquely welcoming for either four for dinner or sixty for cocktails.

Robert A.M. Stern Architects and Brian J. McCarthy, Inc.

IN 2013, clients came to Robert A.M. Stern Architects after buying an additional unit next to their apartment in an architecturally distinguished Park Avenue building designed in 1916 by J. E. R. Carpenter. "The couple asked us to pull out all the stops in the dining room," recalls Stern partner Randy M. Correll. "They wanted a room where they could host large buffets, but also where they would feel comfortable if it was just the two of them." Correll suggested converting an old bedroom and bathroom into the dining room. "That made it a twenty-by-twenty-foot room, so we created a recessed plaster circle in the square in the eleven-foot-tall ceiling," he says. "Then we added pilasters and an over-scaled herringbone floor."

New York designer Brian J. McCarthy did the spare, elegant décor. He commissioned Atelier Mériguet-Carrère for the magnificent molded-plaster bas-relief panels with nature scenes. When they were completed, the Parisian artisans came to Manhattan for a week to install them. They surrounded the panels with persimmon-lacquered frames, laid gold leaf on top of the frames, then scraped off some of the gold. Such tricks add to the magical light that infuses this unforgettable room.

Robert A.M. Stern Architects and MAC II

WHEN ROBERT A.M. STERN ARCHITECTS was completing the luxurious limestone apartment building at 15 Central Park West in 2007, a prominent New York financier bought the entire penthouse floor.

"We were hired by the developers of the building to work with the owner of the apartment while the building was still being built," says Stern partner Roger Seifter. This enabled them to reconfigure the layout of the rooms. For the master bedroom, the client did not want the bed to face directly north or east, so the architects created an ellipse and put it at an angle in order to capture the best panoramic views of Central Park. "We like curves and wanted it to be sexy and sensual," Seifter notes.

The ribbed plaster walls, formed on site, have a corduroy texture that continues up to the thirteen-foot coved, stepped ceiling, to soften the formality of the room. Mica Ertegun of MAC II did the decoration. "I wanted to take advantage of the view and amazing light, which showed off a gleaming New York," Ertegun says. "The addition of a light cove, reeded plaster walls, and pale blue-green palette enhanced the light and its effect on the room throughout the day and into the evening." The process "was quite collaborative: Mica had ideas that melded well with ours," Seifter adds. "It's a fabulous room, especially at night."

Robert A.M. Stern Architects
and S.R. Gambrel

IN 2016, Gary Brewer of Robert A.M. Stern
Architects collaborated with the decorator Steven
Gambrel on a gut renovation of a developer's Park
Avenue apartment in one of Rosario Candela's
most impressive buildings. "Our client wanted her
apartment to present a streamlined and urbane
aesthetic," Brewer says. "Her direction was
traditional with a twist to reflect the contemporary
lifestyle of her family."

The result is the perfect combination of Gambrel's
strong, confident interiors and Stern's impeccable
use of classical architecture. The master bathroom
is especially handsome. Brewer chose a rare lilac
marble for the walls, the bathtub surround, and the
countertops. The light fixture is a Gambrel design
manufactured by The Urban Electric Co. The
mirror over the bathtub is in perfect symmetry with
the window opposite. This is how stylish traditional
can look.

Robert Couturier Inc.

THE MULTITALENTED, French-born, New York–based architect and designer Robert Couturier is very versatile, but rarely is he asked to create, as he puts it, "an 1880s version of a Louis XVI house" in Borough Park, Brooklyn.

In 2010, Couturier took his clients to Paris, and after they visited the Musée Nissim de Camondo, they began to acquire the perfect collection for their new home. This includes the antique pale blue and gray boiseries and marble fireplace, which they acquired from Féau & Cie, the contemporary chandelier, and several other pieces of fine French furniture from Galerie Perrin and other top Parisian antiquaries. Their pale blue salon, with its magnificent Savonnerie hand-knotted carpet, a vintage Lalique glass coffee table, and beautifully embroidered silk curtains, is now a showcase for beautiful pieces, including many important Louis XVI antiques: gilded chairs, commode, desk, and center table. No luxurious detail is lacking—even the mantel has gilt-bronze decoration, as do the Rococo sconces and lyre-shaped firedogs.

Couturier has an encyclopedic knowledge of the arts and architecture of eighteenth-century France, because, as he notes, "I'm completely addicted to luxury." His clients are not far behind; he is now working on a glamorous third project for them.

Robert Couturier Inc.

WHEN A NEW YORK FINANCIER and his wife bought an eight-thousand-square-foot apartment on Fifth Avenue, they asked Robert Couturier to design the dining room with serious boiseries, but with a decided levity and freshness. The space is a confection of old and new, with a combination of contemporary and vintage chairs, tables and lighting, and whimsical palm tree plasterwork and mirrored panels that are offset by lavender silk curtains. The palm trees are actually new confections inspired by nineteenth-century models that once graced the mirrored ballroom of a former Rothschild house in Paris, which is today the residence of the American ambassador to France.

What makes this room modern and glamorous are the highly reflective polished steel amoeba-shaped Ron Arad dining tables, the glass palm tree sconces, and the Karl Springer chairs with Lucite legs. The Eugène Printz ceiling fixture looks like a top that has been launched into space. White cowhide rugs take the seriousness out of the fine, but old-fashioned, parquet floor. The room is like a dream come true.

Robert Kahn Architect

SAINT LOUIS–BORN, New York–based architect Robert Kahn is a man of many talents: he designs residences for some of the most creative people in New York (among them Frank Stella), edits travel guides (the "City Secrets" series), and has a keen social conscience. Years ago, he created sets of blueprints for middle-class people of limited means who wanted to build their own houses without having to hire architects. Their local contractors could use these blueprints and customize them to suit the clients' needs.

In 2017, Kahn completed a Greenwich Village loft for a dancer and her angel investor husband. He reconfigured the space into a duplex, and then spent years with the couple furnishing it with rare vintage pieces, including a pair of Finn Juhl Pelican chairs from 1940 in white lambs' wool, a standing lamp designed in 1947 by J. T. Kalmar, a Pierre Paulin desk from 1952, and a rare pair of orange lounge chairs designed by Carlo Hauner for Forma. The custom chandelier is a contemporary piece by Jeff Zimmerman.

The thirty-foot-long, eighteen-foot-wide living room with its twenty-two-foot ceiling has mahogany walls and a leather-tiled floor bordered in brown travertine marble. The far wall of white-painted brick has ample windows that flood the room in natural light. The spiral staircase and balconies that Kahn designed are steel, covered with auto-body paint. There is a private dance studio on the second floor. The clear beauty of the loft has already been celebrated; it won the apartment category in *Interior Design*'s 2017 NYCxDesign Awards.

S.R. Gambrel

TRAINED AS AN ARCHITECT but a historian by hobby, New York designer Steven Gambrel creates the most textured, traditional, luxurious, and intriguing interiors from scratch. A few years ago, after buying a full-floor apartment in a prewar building on the Upper East Side, a client and his wife visited the bar at the Connaught Hotel in London and started raving about it. Gambrel was delighted; he had already concluded that there was no important architecture left in the apartment, so he gutted it and channeled the Connaught bar.

The living room may not explicitly look like the bar, but the references are easy to see in its dramatic and dark arched entryway, deep-coved lacquered ceiling, crisp new paneling, a pair of immense mirrors, and a neoclassical fireplace surround, which is based on one Gambrel saw in Ireland. The bar is referenced in the room's comfort as well, with its tufted sofa that stretches half its width, large club chairs, and a thick, soft carpet. The palette, mostly pale yellow and gray, is calm and would be suitable in any English-style interior.

Sandra Nunnerley, Inc.

NEW ZEALAND–BORN interior designer Sandra Nunnerley has a background that has served her well, ever since she opened her New York office more than two decades ago. She studied fine art and architecture and worked in the art business in Sydney, Paris, London, and New York. Today, many of her best clients are serious art collectors. The photography collector who owns a prewar Rosario Candela co-op on Park Avenue in Lenox Hill gave Nunnerley full rein to gut the apartment and reconfigure the space with an open plan. "The idea was for people to enjoy the owner's extensive art collection without making it feel museum-like," Nunnerley says. The large living room is purposefully multifunctional: perfect for when the owner is having breakfast with coffee and the papers, watching television, welcoming her grown children, or entertaining large groups for her charities. Against walls lined in beige linen, Nunnerley mounted African masks next to black-and-white ceramic sculptures by the contemporary artist Maren Kloppmann and groupings of photographs by André Kertész, Ruth Bernhard, Todd Hido, and Joel Shapiro. Nunnerley designed the black slate fireplace, the shimmering silk and wool rug, and the snakeskin ottoman. The room is serene, glamorous, and, as Nunnerley proudly says, "very comfortable."

ATRIUM DINING

Sawyer | Berson

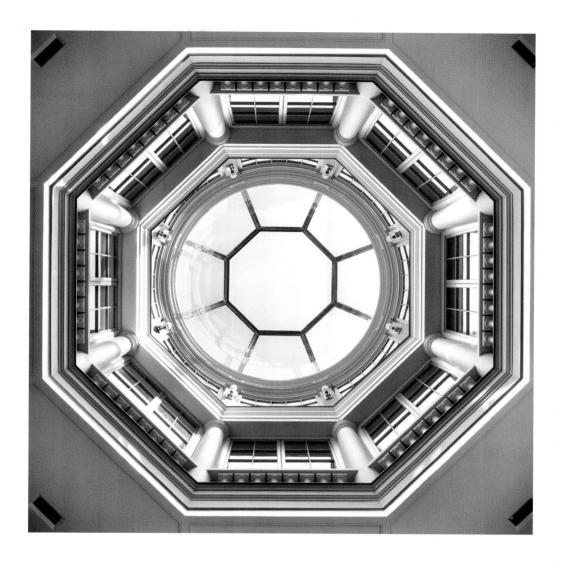

IN 1999, when a young New York–born financier returned to Manhattan after working in the Far East, he bought a handsome seventeen-thousand-square-foot, Federal-style town house on the Upper East Side. The landmarked residence had been designed for a couple in 1923 by favorite society architects Cross & Cross (Sister Parish grew up in a Cross & Cross mansion.)

For years, the bachelor happily puttered around the six-story building, which had belonged to renegade British financier James Goldsmith in the 1980s. Then the New Yorker met his wife, they married, she had a baby, and they hired Sawyer | Berson, the New York architecture and design firm, to renovate and reconfigure the house to make it more family friendly. It took five years (four more babies arrived during the process), and the results are spectacular. The double-height dining room is now a soaring atrium bathed in natural light from a new octagonal skylight. The eight clerestory windows are actually two-way mirrors to let light into the baths and dressing rooms behind them. Brian Sawyer says he replaced a covered airshaft with "the most extravagant oculus" (brought in by crane) and installed detailed classical cornices and paneling. The decoration of the room, completed in 2012, includes a Georgian-style marble mantelpiece designed by Sawyer | Berson and fabricated by Chesneys; eighteenth- and early nineteenth-century English and French antiques sourced at top dealers like Mallett, Kentshire, Philip Colleck, and Jonathan Burden; and an antique Agra rug from Mansour. The owner's Japanese ink paintings hang on walls covered in raw silk the color of celadon, a perfect foil for the purple mantel.

Sawyer | Berson and Pierce Allen

INSTALLING AN INDOOR POOL in the basement of a six-story, 1841 brick town house is quite a feat of engineering. In 2011, Brian Sawyer, of the New York architecture and design firm Sawyer | Berson, orchestrated this particular one on East 11th Street in Greenwich Village just off Fifth Avenue. It required a major excavation, including the underpinning of the adjacent town houses with twenty-foot-tall concrete retaining walls that enclosed the lower level of the house. The stainless-steel shell of the pool was then placed at the back of the house next to the garden, where it could get natural light. (Sawyer is also a landscape architect.)

Today, of course, none of this effort is evident, but the architects created the perfect shell for interior designer DD Allen of Pierce Allen to conceive a spectacular, exotic room. "This was a major team effort," Allen says. "The client is a frequent traveler, and he would often come home with design ideas from exotic places, so we did a Santorini room, a safari room, a yacht room, an English men's club, and, for the pool, a Moroccan room." Allen embraced the Moroccan theme. "The embroidery patterns on the textiles, the wall tiles, the niches, and lanterns were all inspired by trips to Morocco," she says. She had the walls and plaster ceiling waterproofed (by an old Moroccan technique), added niches, commissioned glass lamps from Venice, and installed Moroccan shutters, Moroccan leather poufs, and a Moroccan rug. She is happy to say the athletic owners swim there year round.

Selldorf Architects

IN 2008, a mother with two daughters bought two floors in a former YMCA on West 23rd Street in Chelsea. The upper floor had been a running track; the lower, basketball courts. The challenge was to convert the fifty-nine-hundred-square-foot space into a three-bedroom duplex.

"I believe that residential projects are a form of portraiture and should develop out of a deep understanding of the individual needs and desires of the client—balanced, of course, against the constraints of existing conditions, context, program, and budget," says Annabelle Selldorf, principal of the New York firm she founded in 1988. "That way the design evolves almost intuitively and is specific and reflective." The key decision here was to take the place apart, removing the interior walls on the mezzanine floor and installing handsome new sash windows throughout. The upper floor, with its dark blue tiles, has an open kitchen, dining area, and lounge. (Selldorf designed the banquette and large walnut table.) The lower floor has bedrooms, an office, and a living room with a colorful sectional sofa by the Italian artist and designer Gaetano Pesce.

Revealing her attitude about reconfiguring old buildings, one of her great strengths (think of the Neue Galerie in New York and the Clark Art Institute in Williamstown, Massachusetts), Selldorf says, "With historic preservation projects, the challenge is always to consider which aspects of the original to keep, which to modify, and where to insert new interventions so there's a seamless whole at the end." This loft is a masterful example of all that.

Shelton Mindel

WHEN A CLIENT bought a glass-ceilinged and glass-curtain-walled duplex penthouse in Pritzker Prize–winning architect Jean Nouvel's first Manhattan apartment building, at 40 Mercer Street, he naturally went to New York's preeminent modernist residential architect, Lee F. Mindel. Why? Mindel is a master at integrating architecture, interior design, and landscape. His firm, Shelton Mindel, has been internationally acclaimed since its founding in 1978. The firm has won more than thirty AIA (American Institute of Architects) awards as well as the prestigious Cooper-Hewitt National Design Award for Interior Design (in 2011). Mindel designs homewares as well: outdoor seating for Sutherland Furniture, rugs for V'Soske, chairs for Knoll, and bathroom fixtures and lighting for Waterworks.

For the duplex, Mindel built a two-story slatted white floating cube encompassing the master bedroom suite and a study. Beneath it is the kitchen and, next to it, the dining room with extensive city views on three sides. The architect is a longtime connoisseur and collector of fine Scandinavian modern furniture, which explains the Poul Henningsen Artichoke lamp (this one a custom model with glass leaves instead of metal ones), the Poul Kjærholm expandable table, and the lime-green Arne Jacobsen chairs. Adding to the outside-inside feeling is a rug from V'Soske that was custom woven to simulate grass.

AERIE WITH FOUR VIEWS

Shelton Mindel and Reed A. Morrison

NEW YORK ARCHITECT Lee F. Mindel bought the top floor of a midtown manufacturing building in 1994 because it offered panoramic views on four sides—you could see all the way from the East River to the Hudson.

In converting the main floor into an apartment, Mindel, architect Reed A. Morrison, and Mindel's late business partner, architect Peter Shelton, were most concerned about keeping the public volumes open, both for the views and to let light penetrate deep into the apartment. The foyer is a rotunda with an eye-catcher: a steel staircase that twists in two directions, like an S, as it ascends to the dramatic, flat-topped, glass-enclosed roof pavilion Mindel designed—a true urban folly.

YANKEE INGENUITY

Stephanie Stokes, Inc.

LIKE MANY SOPHISTICATED New York decorators, Stephanie Stokes frequently travels to Europe to scout antiques and art for clients (and for herself). In 1989, she visited the venerable London dealer Mallett, where she found an eighteenth-century English four-poster with eleven-foot-tall carved mahogany posts and a magnificent gilt-wood serpentine crown. She coveted it, but she could not afford it (the price was $1 million). She scoured the English countryside for a cheaper alternative without luck, but after returning to New York, she found an important pair of George III carved posts in the basement of Hyde Park Antiques. She bought them in ninety seconds.

"Buying a reproduction four-poster would have been like buying a zircon instead of a diamond," she says. "So then the work began: we proceeded to create a practical American version of the bed with the beauty of the English one. It took nine tradesmen—woodworkers, gilders, mattress makers, upholsterers, you name it. We cut the antique poles and replaced the base with one that could accommodate storage boxes, and we added height above the carving to balance the proportions. Now the crown touches my ten-foot ceiling." It was not at all easy. "Creating the carved crown was a graduate course in decorating," Stokes admits. "To make it serpentine, we had to soak the wood for several months to be able to bend it. Then it was carved and gilded with 24-karat gold leaf." She later designed formal bed hangings with 180 yards of silk, miles of trim, and English chintz.

Why build a four-poster? "It's a room within a room," Stokes explains. "It's a glamorous, inviting sanctuary." It is also accompanied by a perfect selection of antiques: an American mahogany serving table, made in New York circa 1810, and a Louis XVI chest of drawers from France.

A GENTLEMAN'S OASIS

Stephanie Stokes, Inc.

IN 1993 Stephanie Stokes decorated an Upper East Side apartment for a successful (and very dapper) entrepreneur. He gave her a tall order: the most important room would be the one that functioned as a dressing room, a private retreat for making business calls, and an oasis to watch television or read a book. But the room was only three hundred square feet. Stokes, a genius at storage, did a meticulous survey of the man's wardrobe. She installed a wall of cabinets, with four sets of doors that open to sections designated for suits, jackets, and trousers. She added drawers for socks and, in the baseboard, shoes. She retrofitted a Regency side cabinet to store gloves, watches, and cufflinks. When the doors are closed, the client can relax in a striped club chair by the neoclassical working fireplace that Stokes commissioned. The television is hidden in a Sheraton linen press. The Christopher Hyland hand-blocked wallpaper gives the space coziness and continuity.

Stephen Sills Associates

OF ALL THE SUCCESSFUL DECORATORS working in New York today, Stephen Sills is one of the most knowledgeable connoisseurs of European antiques. For the small sitting room on top of a Francophile client's triplex penthouse on Fifth Avenue, Sills took his cue from the Frick Collection, which the adjoining terrace overlooks.

Sills is renowned for his restrained palette: here he painted the walls the same warm gray as the exterior of the Frick, with horizontal indentations to make them look like granite. The white linen curtains and summertime slipcovers add crispness to the scheme. Together they form a quiet background for an Art Deco bust by Raymond Delamarre, a drawing by Salvador Dalí, and a few choice antiques. The vintage Jean-Michel Frank parchment cabinet and nesting tables are the ultimate in refinement, as are the gilded bronze boxes on the coffee table. They were made by twentieth-century French artist Line Vautrin, affectionately known as "the poetess of metal."

Steven Harris Architects and Rees Roberts + Partners

VETERAN TRIBECA ARCHITECT (and Yale School of Architecture professor) Steven Harris is renowned for his ability to reconfigure raw spaces in unconventional ways. For the owner of this Tribeca triplex penthouse, in 2012 Harris and his colleague Eliot Lee were able to get permission from the city's building department to remove a sizeable portion of the second floor, giving them a double-height media room that is twenty-one feet high. Then they commissioned the nineteen-foot-square window, a feat of engineering. They had it fabricated in six large panes of German glass, exactly to the inch of what could be accommodated in the freight elevator of the building. The second feat of engineering is the stair Lee designed. The leather-clad cantilevered treads support rods anchored above them, creating a sculptural piece from which shadows bounce on the wall in an ever-changing configuration as the sun moves. The stairs lead to an upstairs kitchen, dining room, and formal living room and, above that, on the roof, to a breathtaking covered glass porch, complete with an outdoor garden.

Harris's partner, the interior designer Lucien Rees Roberts, furnished the room sparely but with a curator's eye. The rug is silk, the cork coffee table is vintage Paul McCobb, and the delicate vintage wooden armchair is the Dinamarquesa, a much-sought-after model created in 1959 by the Polish-born Brazilian designer Jorge Zalszupin.

Steven Harris Architects and Rees Roberts + Partners

IN 2015, when New York architect Steven Harris and his partner, interior designer Lucien Rees Roberts, were asked to build and decorate a new duplex penthouse on top of a historical building in Tribeca, they faced a dilemma. The building, on Harrison Street, was high enough to see the redbrick tower of the old Mercantile Exchange, but the building's tall parapet blocked much of the rest of the view. Their solution? They simply raised the floor level four feet. This allowed them to put a deep layer of earth on the roof, so they could plant honey locust, Fuji cherry, and hornbeam trees, install a reflecting pool, and create an area for outdoor dining. "The trees and the pool transform the space, giving it a sense of energy," Rees Roberts says. The tracks for the sliding glass doors are just below floor level, so the living room opens seamlessly to the terrace.

The inside-outside sensibility is further enhanced by the use of the limestone pavers throughout (inside they are heated underneath). Rees Roberts custom designed all the furniture, including the eleven-foot-long dining table. He commissioned Ian Engberg, a Brooklyn-based craftsman, to make it with jacaranda veneers from the 1960s. "We had an ideal client, who gave us the freedom to do what we wanted," Rees Roberts says. And the client was smart enough to trust the talented team.

Steven Harris Architects and Rees Roberts + Partners

WHEN ARCHITECT STEVEN HARRIS was asked by a young family to do a complete renovation of an uptown Manhattan town house a few years ago, he suggested adding a two-story addition in the rear, with a wall of casement windows facing the garden. The living room on the balcony upstairs would then overlook the space and the outdoors. The new room was turned into a library, which Harris's colleague, Lucien Rees Roberts, decorated with a pair of comfortable Milo Baughman swivel lounge chairs, an important vintage Jorge Zalszupin wood armchair that Harris discovered in Brazil, and a thick Moroccan rug. The room is twenty-one feet tall, so Harris designed a steel fireplace hood that reaches to the ceiling. "I wanted it to be slightly asymmetrical so the light would hit it in an amazing way," he says. "The planes are all slightly tilted." It is like a soaring sculpture, an ode to space.

A CITY HAVEN

Tino Zervudachi & Associés

ANYONE WHO STROLLS around the periphery of the Palais-Royal in Paris will find themselves struck by the elegant window displays of Galerie Tino Zervudachi, which showcases antiques, vintage furniture, lighting, mirrors, and contemporary works of art by the owner's twin sister, Manuela. It is a treasure house that reflects Zervudachi's own eclectic, refined taste.

Based in Paris but with offices in London and New York, in 2009, Zervudachi decided to buy a pied-à-terre on the Upper East Side. He found an apartment in Barbizon 63, the landmarked building on 63rd and Lexington built in 1926 as the Barbizon Hotel for Women, which hosted many famous tenants over the years, including Joan Crawford, Grace Kelly, Candice Bergen, Liza Minnelli, and Sylvia Plath (Plath's best-selling novel *The Bell Jar* references the hotel). Zervudachi bought the apartment because he liked the exposures on three sides and the intriguing views of bustling midtown. But the living room was long and narrow, so, he explains, "To shorten it, I built bookshelves on opposite sides and installed a long banquette between them for reading and lounging." To add warmth, he lined the walls with caramel-colored Japanese rice paper, after having discovered this medium while working in Japan. "I love the rough edges of the squares," he says, and they definitely make an inviting background for his contemporary paintings.

"This is not an apartment for entertaining—it is for me," he declares. And, fittingly, there is not a reproduction in sight. Zervudachi is into authenticity. Everything is antique, vintage, or custom made for the space.

Tom Britt

AFTER FIVE DECADES creating spectacular interiors for an international clientele, Kansas-born Tom Britt remains the brashest, funniest, and most wonderfully talented of all Manhattan's decorators. His style is unique: he boldly produces fabulous, theatrical interiors for others and himself.

In his three-floor apartment in an Upper East Side town house built in 1902, Britt lives like a pasha. His grand salon, known as the Blue Room, is designed for theatrical nighttime entertaining: walls covered with aubergine lacquer and mirrored boiseries, twenty-five-foot-tall ceilings boasting elaborate white plasterwork, and chic black floors. Chandeliers, spotlights, and candles pick out the gold of the black Regency armchairs, porphyry busts of Roman emperors, sang-de-boeuf Chinese vases, and a wall full of antique bird engravings from the collection of another over-the-top Manhattan decorator, the late Rose Cumming.

This truly is one of the most glamorous rooms in New York—dramatic, exotic, and magical.

SEAMLESS COMPOSITION

Tsao & McKown

THE CENTRAL PARK WEST duplex of New York architects and designers
Calvin Tsao and Zack McKown is modern but wonderfully eclectic, with
antique fabrics, vintage lighting, and a few select pieces of furniture. One side
of the sleek living room is lined with silver-leafed panels that hide cupboard
space (the apartment is "all about storage," Tsao notes). The shimmering silver
also bounces natural light onto the golden Venetian gondolier torches, cushions
covered with Javanese wedding textiles, and a large Sicilian cross. The splayed
Napoleon III stools are covered in a colorful fabric depicting Masonic symbols.

The room is serene, sensuous, beautifully composed, and a true sanctuary in the
middle of bustling Manhattan.

Vera Blinken

CERTAIN PEOPLE ARE BLESSED with an exceptional eye for art, like Donald M. Blinken, the investment banker and former United States ambassador to Hungary. Living in New York in the late 1950s, Blinken was an early follower of the New York School of art and often visited Mark Rothko's West 60th Street studio in Manhattan. Eventually, when Rothko came to trust Blinken's deep commitment to his art, he let Blinken buy three important oils, which are now the crowning glory of his and his wife Vera's co-op on the East River. "We needed a big room for those paintings, one that had real scale," he says.

Vera Blinken, a Hungarian who trained with Edward Durell Stone before becoming a decorator, chose a luminous, honey-toned ivory as background for the Rothkos. She designed the sleek upholstered settee, benches, and armless chairs in peach, so virtually nothing distracts from the monumental paintings. After Rothko's suicide in 1976, Mr. Blinken was appointed chairman of the Mark Rothko Foundation.

Victoria Hagan Interiors and Peter Pennoyer Architects

IN 1998, when a couple with five children bought a seven-story town house built in 1872 in Lenox Hill, they presented New York architect Peter Pennoyer and decorator Victoria Hagan with a unique situation. Its former owner had gutted the house. "It was down to the floor decks, so we essentially built a new house," Pennoyer says. The seventh floor, the top floor of a penthouse that was added later, has three exposures and is flooded with daylight. It became the music room, where the husband played the piano while the children gathered on the sofa. "The melody of the room was set by the grand piano," Hagan says. "Everything was black and white and graphic."

The minimalist room in turn became the media room, complete with a movie screen that descends from the ceiling and blackout curtains that drop at the push of a button. "Because there was no set formula for the room, the clients were open to fun new things, such as the contemporary chaise and the vintage Lucite chairs," Hagan says. "Then I added a soft shaggy carpet, so you relax the moment you step into the room and your feet sink into it." Pennoyer installed classical moldings in other rooms, but not on this floor. "I felt it should feel like an addition from the 1930s," he explains. (The sleek, massive black granite fireplace surround he designed is clearly Deco-inspired.) "It is unusual for us to design a room with no moldings; here it is all about the proportions."

ACKNOWLEDGMENTS

FIRST, I WANT TO EXPRESS my warmest appreciation for all the architects and interior designers whose kind forbearance allowed me to interview them and record their extraordinary rooms. Each is an artist who knows how to adapt his or her singular style to suit a client. In Leo Tolstoy's treatise of 1897, *What Is Art?*, the author ponders art as "an activity by means of which one man, having experienced a feeling, intentionally transmits it to others." This is just what these talents do, in spades. Tolstoy added, "The recipient of a truly artistic impression is so united to the artist that he feels as if the work were his own and not someone else's." That is, without the smart homeowners who sought out and inspired these creative men and women—not to mention funding them—the rooms in this book would not exist.

Nor would they have happened without the passion, patience, and dogged determination of the designers. It is doubly difficult to realize projects in New York. There are city permits to obtain and strict safety codes to comply with—and that is before confronting the rules of individual apartment buildings. Most of the best ones allow major construction only between Memorial Day and Labor Day, which requires an accelerated schedule and a genius sequencing of tasks. To accomplish the level of work chronicled in this book requires brilliance, expertise, and, yes, often sheer charm.

On the more personal side, I am especially indebted to David Morton, the former associate publisher of Rizzoli International Publications, who commissioned this book, and to my dear friend Suzanne Stephens, deputy editor at *Architectural Record* magazine, who introduced us years ago. I'm also deeply thankful for the contributions of Rizzoli publisher Charles Miers, gifted book designer Henry Connell, and the amiable production manager Alyn Evans. Philip Reeser, the brave editor who guided me tirelessly but always with good humor after David Morton retired, has my everlasting gratitude and friendship. And I am most obliged to architect Robert A.M. Stern, who, in my opinion, is "Mr. New York," for contributing a foreword.

I have nothing but the greatest admiration for the exceptionally skilled photographers, many of whom I have known for decades, who contributed ideas as well as their amazing work to this book—and their agents and representatives, who patiently guided me through the lengthy permissions process.

And finally I would like to tip my hat to my indefatigable cheerleading squad: my family, my friends Stacy McLaughlin, Val Slosky, Suzanne Charlé, Cathleen McGuigan, Connie Shuman, Anne Kriken Mann, Susan Bennett, Laila Young, the late Cheryl Merser, and former colleagues at *Town & Country*, *House & Garden*, *Architectural Digest*, 1stdibs.com, and the *New York Times* who provided me with the on-the-job training that made this book possible. Years ago my Paris friend Souren Melikian told me that life is not long enough to pursue art, architecture, and design as a weekend hobby; writing about these subjects has to be a full-time job. How lucky was I to be able to follow his advice!

PHOTOGRAPHY CREDITS

Eric Piasecki / OTTO: 2

Durston Saylor / *Architectural Digest* © Condé Nast: 8

Photography by Julian Schnabel. © Julian Schnabel Studio: 11

Lizzie Himmel: 12

Peter Aaron / OTTO: 14–15

Photography by Paolo Petrignani. Courtesy of Achille Salvagni: 16, 17

Michel Arnaud: 18, 19

Martyn Thompson / Trunk Archive: 20, 21

Richard Powers / Powershot: 23

Michael Mundy © 2018. Represented by www.traffic-nyc.com: 24

John M. Hall: 26–27

Durston Saylor / *Architectural Digest* © Condé Nast: 28–29

Michel Arnaud: 30–31, 32–33

Photography by Fritz von der Schulenburg. Courtesy of Bunny Williams: 34–35, 35

Pieter Estersohn: 36–37

Photography by Giorgio Baroni. Courtesy of Cabinet Alberto Pinto: 38, 39

Photography by Jacques Pépion. Courtesy of Cabinet Alberto Pinto: 40, 41, 42–43, 44, 45

Stephen Kent Johnson / OTTO: 46, 47, 48–49

Pieter Estersohn: 50, 50–51

Eric Piasecki / OTTO: 52–53

Jason Schmidt: 54–55

Pieter Estersohn: 56–57

Eric Piasecki / OTTO: 58

Durston Saylor / *Architectural Digest* © Condé Nast: 60–61

Scott Frances / OTTO: 62–63

Durston Saylor: 64–65, 66, 67, 68, 69, 70–71

DBOX: 72–73

Oberto Gili / *House & Garden* © Condé Nast: 74–75

James Ewing / OTTO: 76–77, 77, 78–79

© 2018 Judd Foundation / Artists Rights Society (ARS), New York: 76–77, 77, 78–79

© 2018 David Novros / Artists Rights Society (ARS), New York: 76–77, 77

Mark Roskams: 80, 81, 82–83

Durston Saylor: 84, 86–87

Annie Schlechter: 85

Paul Warchol: 88–89, 90, 91, 92–93, 94–95, 96, 96–97, 98–99, 100–01

Ben Hoffmann: 102–03

Photography by T. Whitney Cox. Courtesy of Georgis & Mirgorodsky: 104–05, 105

Michael Moran / OTTO: 106–07

Horst P. Horst / Condé Nast Collection / Getty Images: 108–09, 109

Courtesy of GLUCK+: 110

Paul Warchol: 111

Durston Saylor: 112, 113, 114–15

Mick Hales: 116–17, 118–19

Diego Giacometti © 2018 Artists Rights Society (ARS), New York / ADAGP, Paris: 118–19

Tria Giovan: 120, 122–23, 124–25, 126–27

Nick Johnson: 128–29, 130–31

William Waldron / OTTO: 132, 133

Peter Aaron / OTTO: 134–35

Michael Mundy © 2018. Represented by www.traffic-nyc.com: 136–37

Durston Saylor / *Architectural Digest* © Condé Nast: 138–39

Michael Moran / OTTO: 140–41, 142–43

Photography by Francesco Lagnese. Courtesy of Joanne De Palma: 144, 145, 146, 147

Lizzie Himmel: 148, 148–49

René and Barbara Stoeltie: 150, 151, 152–53

Durston Saylor: 154, 155, 156–57

Durston Saylor / *Architectural Digest* © Condé Nast: 158–59, 160, 161

First published in the United States of America in 2018 by
Rizzoli International Publications, Inc.
300 Park Avenue South
New York, NY 10010
www.rizzoliusa.com

Copyright © 2018 Wendy Moonan
ISBN: 978-0-8478-4635-1
Library of Congress Control Number: 2018938669

For Rizzoli International Publications:
Philip Reeser, Editor
Alyn Evans, Production Manager
Elizabeth Smith, Copy Editor

Design: Henry Connell
Printed in China
2018 2019 2020 2021 / 10 9 8 7 6 5 4 3 2 1